THE DAME CECILY SPUME DRAMA NOTEBOOK

The Dame Cecily Spume

DRAMA NOTEBOOK

Using sketches by

NICK PAGE

MINSTREL
Eastbourne

First published 1990

*Cover design and text illustrations
by Russell Davies*

British Library Cataloguing in Publication Data

Page, Nick
The Dame Cecily Spume drama notebook.
I. Title
822.914

ISBN 1–85424–097–8

Printed in Great Britain for
Minstrel, an imprint of Monarch Publications Ltd
1 St Anne's Road, Eastbourne, E Sussex BN21 3UN by
Richard Clay Ltd, Bungay, Suffolk
Typeset by J&L Composition Ltd, Filey, North Yorkshire

CONTENTS

ABBREVIATIONS OF STAGE DIRECTIONS

CS	Centre Stage	SL	Stage Left
DS	Downstage	SR	Stage Right
DSC	Downstage centre	US	Upstage
DSL	Downstage left	USC	Upstage centre
DSR	Downstage right	USL	Upstage left
OS	Offstage	USR	Upstage right

PERFORMING LICENCE

All amateur groups performing at non-profit-making events are welcome to use the sketches in this book without charge. Please not however that photocopying of the text is not allowed without permission in writing from the publishers.

Any other group wishing to perform should contact Nick Page at the following address for a licence:

Nick Page
c/o Oasis
Haddon Hall Baptist Church
Tower Bridge Road
London SE1 4TR

FOREWORD

I was first introduced to Dame Cecily Spume several years ago, when I was an actor and writer with Ambush Theatre Company. Her sister Daphne was then editor of our magazine, *The Ambush Sketchbook*. Dame Cecily was kind enough to take an interest in our work and, over the course of our professional career, gave us much help, advice and encouragement. I am honoured that she should have chosen my sketches as the basis of her training method.

On the whole they are basically simple, straight forward, funny sketches. If there's one message or 'point' that seems to recur it's simply that God loves you. I suppose that seems a bit naive, but I believe it's a message that is as relevant today as it was when Jesus said it. If the sketches can, through laughter, help people understand a bit more about God and his love for us, then this book will have been worthwhile.

Two of the sketches were written by Roger Porthouse, a frequent contributor to *The Ambush Sketchbook* and a fellow Spume student. My thanks go to him for letting me include them, and the cheque's in the post.

Along with Dame Cecily, I'd like to thank the members of Ambush Theatre Company for all their hard work, for putting up with me when I was being a 'writer', and for not criticising *too* much. My thanks to Paul, Heather, David, Carol, Tim and, especially, to my wife, Claire for her constant love and support.

Nick Page

INTRODUCTION

Do you want to produce great Christian theatre?

Do you want to be the greatest actor of your generation?

Do you want to act in the West End, appear in films and win BAFTA awards?

Then you need the *Dame Cecily Spume Drama Method!*

This simple, trustworthy method can transform you overnight into a Christian actor of such stature that people will talk of Kenneth Branagh as being the next you!

Some of our testimonials:

> I used to be a real ham actor, but now I'm world famous.
>
> *Jack N. of Esher, Surrey.*

> Before using the Dame Cecily Spume method I was hideously ugly with all the acting ability of a small hairbrush. Now I'm the best film actress in the world.
>
> *Meryl S. of Nottingham.*

> You were wonderful, lovey!
>
> *Sir John G. of Accrington, Lancs.*

These are just a few of the many satisfied actors and actresses who have used the *Dame Cecily Spume Drama Method*, developed several years ago by that great Dame of the theatre, to incorporate the best of the more complicated schools of theatre pioneered by such luminaries as Stanislavski, Lee Strasburg or Brian Clough. Not only do you feel thoroughly prepared as a character therefore, but you also get to play at Wembley.

Dame Cecily says:

My system is very easy to learn, but has helped many famous actors. It is based on the idea that all theatre is very simple and can be reduced to a few easily remembered 'rules'. All you have to do is remember the following:

1 Remember the words.
2 Remember the movements.
3 Remember who you're supposed to be playing.
4 Remember, remember the fifth of November.[1]

With those simple rules at your command, the world of theatre is your oyster. You can play any part from King Lear to King Kong. You too can be lionised, hero-worshipped and generally admired.

I have put together this book as a training course. Using some of the sketches by a little-known hack-writer, you will learn about group work, two-handers, rehearsals and much, much more.

Treat this book with care—it is a doorway into the world of great acting.

---

[1] This rule optional.

THE DAME CECILY SPUME DRAMA METHOD

Actors are a funny breed. Like thoroughbred race-horses, they are nervous, touchy and hugely talented. Also, they smell the same.

I started teaching in 1927. Many would visit my Hampstead studio and, after a course of lessons which would change their lives, double their talent and leave their washing whiter than white, they would urge me to put pen to paper. 'Cecily,' they would say, 'write it down!'

Now, some seventy years later, I have decided to

share my insights with the nation. I find that I have distilled all my experience into four rules:

1 Remember the words.
2 Remember the movements.
3 Remember who you're supposed to be playing.
4 Remember, remember the fifth of November.[1]

Most mistakes on stage arise from forgetting one or more of these rules (although rarely no. 4). Forgetting the words is known as 'drying'. Forgetting the movements is known as 'standing still and not doing anything'. Forgetting who you're supposed to be playing is known as 'I'm stuck in a hideous nightmare'. Forgetting all three is known as 'complete amnesia'.

I realise these are technical terms, but, rest assured, any layman with the IQ of a small toad can understand the theory. Unfortunately that rules out estate agents, so if you are an estate agent I should go and get your money back.

The important thing is to *perform*. That's why I decided to use Mr Page's sketches. The nice people who produced this book thought they might come in useful to many church drama groups. You can, if you have a sort of dramatic suicidal tendency, just use this book as a book of sketches. But you will miss out on my method and, therefore, the chance of being a hugely famous actor.

---

[1] This rule still optional.

LESSON ONE
REHEARSALS

These are absolutely crucial. I mean, when else are you going to hear the latest gossip?

For a rehearsal to be successful it must contain one crucial element—coffee. And lots of it. This is so you can have that most creative of times, the coffee break. After all, most of the great shows I have been involved in have been knocked together over a cup of the old Gold Blend. I remember dearest Noël once wrote an entire revue whilst dunking his rich tea biscuit.

In my opinion, rehearsals are largely overrated. Apart

from having a good natter and a nice cup of coffee they don't seem to be entirely necessary. I know there's a modern school of thought which says that you should get your sketches as good as they possibly can be, but the audience will never know how good they might have been anyway. What you've never had, you never miss.

Save yourself a lot of bother. All you have to do is follow the four rules of my method and Bob, as they say, is the brother of your father!

LESSON TWO
GROUP WORK

Only one thing is essential for vibrant, thrilling, exciting group work. A group.

I know that seems a bit obvious, but you'd be amazed at how many people have tried to do group work with only one person. I'll never forget the day darling Larry showed me his Richard III, with only him in it. I said to him, 'Larry, it's wonderful, but don't you think it could be so much better with more people in it?' I'll never forget the look of childlike wonder on his face when he grasped this concept. It was as if a great load had been taken off his back. After that, he never looked back.

So there you have it. If you're going to do any of the pieces that follow make sure there are enough of you. People say to me, 'Cecily! How many people do you need for a group?' and my answer is nearly always the same.

'It all depends,' I say. And that seems to satisfy them.

My own personal preference is that a group should be not less than three and not more than quite a lot more than three. The cast list is usually a good guide.

Wally the Prat

Characters: WALLY PRATT—a well meaning, unfashionable wally.
ERICA—the narrator.
SADIE—a bimbo.
CLARKE—a cool dude.

Plot: The good Samaritan. WALLY is universally regarded as an idiot. Nevertheless, he is the only one who helps CLARKE when he is in trouble. However, this only brings WALLY more criticism and ridicule.

Main Point: That what a person looks like is not what he is.

Running Time: 10 minutes.

Suitability: Evangelistic, teenagers.

Staging: The cast are all onstage. CLARKE stands SR, WALLY and ERICA CS and SADIE SL.

Props/Costumes: WALLY wears little glasses, flared trousers and an anorak. He has a pair of binoculars. ERICA carries a notebook and pencil. SADIE wears a pair of extremely high heels and a vacuous expression. CLARKE carries a comb which he uses with monotonous regularity. You also need a note which is passed to CLARKE.

Remarks: All cast are on stage. When they are not involved in the action they simply turn away from the audience and freeze. 'Entering' therefore involves turning and moving.

[ERICA *steps forward CS.* WALLY *is standing CS facing audience, a silly grin fixed on his face.*]

ERICA: [*To audience*] This is Wally.

WALLY: [*Coming to life and waving to audience*] Hello.

ERICA: He wears flares, and an anorak, and says things like—

WALLY: Blinking flip!

ERICA: And

WALLY: Crikey!

ERICA: Oh yeah, Wally's a real hero. Don't believe me? Pin your ears back and listen. See—this is my school—Saint Neanderthal's Comprehensive . . .

WALLY: [*Interrupting*] Hello Erica.

[*He comes up to* ERICA, *standing annoyingly close. Throughout the sketch, he does this to everybody he talks to. He is always standing too close to them.*]

ERICA: [*To* WALLY, *pushing him away*] Hi Wally.

WALLY: What are you doing?

ERICA: I'm just trying to narrate a story.

WALLY: Oh, who's it about?

ERICA: It's about a wally.

WALLY: Oh, that's my name. Wally—Wally Pratt. [*He laughs annoyingly*] That's a coincidence isn't it?

ERICA: Yes. Isn't it just.

WALLY: I like a good coincidence. Guess what happened to me over the weekend.

ERICA: Let me see . . . you bought a new Bonnie Langford record.

WALLY: No.

ERICA: You went to your rafia mat-making classes.

WALLY: Wrong.

ERICA: You went out and got incredibly drunk and joined the foreign legion.

WALLY: Yes. [*Pause*] That was a joke actually.

ERICA: I'd never have guessed.

WALLY: I saw a lesser-spotted lump warbler!

ERICA: You didn't!

WALLY: I did! The first one of spring.

ERICA: What is a lesser-spotted lump warbler?

WALLY: A bird. Very rare. I won a £50 prize from 'Bird-Spotters Weekly' for spotting it. Do you want to hear how it all happened?

ERICA: No. Go away.

WALLY: Lucky I know you don't mean that. Well, I was down by the reservoir . . .

[*He holds the binoculars up and looks in the direction of* SADIE *SR. Seeing* SADIE *has a marked effect on him.*]

WALLY: Oooooooohhh!

ERICA: Pardon?

WALLY: Ooooh! There she is. Isn't she beautiful?

ERICA: That's Sadie.

WALLY: I know

ERICA: Wally, you're in love!

WALLY: Oooooh!

ERICA: Look—you just sigh for a minute, I'll explain a bit more to the audience. [*To audience*] Sadie Buxom is the most sought-after girl in the school . . .

SADIE: [*Interrupting*] You narrating?

ERICA: [*To* SADIE] I'm trying to.

SADIE: Don't forget to tell them I want to be a model.

[*She walks up and down between SR and CS, showing off her 'modelling'*.]

ERICA: [*To audience*] Sadie wants to be a model. She wants to wear beautiful clothes, and break men's hearts. That's why she walks around like a constipated heron. And here we find Wally is in love with her.

[WALLY *sidles up close to* SADIE.]

WALLY: Hello Sadie.

SADIE: [*Pushing him away, not interested*] Hi.

WALLY: Er . . . do you want to come and see my Bonnie Langford poster?

SADIE: You what?

WALLY: Nothing.

SADIE: You are such a wally, Wally.

WALLY: [*Summoning up courage*] Sadie, you wouldn't like to go out with me would you?

SADIE: Correct.

WALLY: Pardon?

SADIE: Wally—I would prefer to be thrown into a crocodile infested cesspit than go out with you. I'd . . . I'd rather have to go behind the bicycle sheds!

[*The rest of the cast sing some dramatic chords*.]

ERICA: [*To audience*] Yes! The worst fate that can befall anyone here at Saint Neanderthal's is to have to go behind the bicycle sheds.

[*They sing dramatic chords again*.]

ERICA: [*To audience*] There the school villain, known as the Big Boss, holds court. And if the Big Boss wants to see you, you know what will happen to you—your teeth start chattering, your knees knock, your bile duct starts to wobble up and down, you start to sweat . . .

SADIE: [*To* ERICA) Oi! Can we continue with our scene please?

ERICA: [*To* SADIE] Oh. Right. Carry on.

SADIE: [*To* WALLY] So you see, it's just not on.
WALLY: Oh. What's wrong with me then?
SADIE: You have greasy hair, terminal dandruff, acne, glasses and you wear clothes no decent self-respecting tramp would be seen dead in.
WALLY: But apart from that . . .
SADIE: You're a wally.
WALLY: But I love you.
SADIE: Well of course you do! It's tragic, but men feel that way about me.

[*She turns away and freezes.* WALLY *returns to* ERICA *CS.*]

WALLY: [*To* ERICA] What did I do wrong?
ERICA: No luck?
WALLY: I told her I loved her.
ERICA: Oh Wally! You don't love people these days, Wally, you treat them with contempt. [*To audience*] So, you see, Wally has a few problems in life . . .
WALLY: [*Interrupting*] Tell them I have a few problems in life.
ERICA: I'm just telling them! I wish everyone would let me get on narrating in peace. As I was saying . . .
WALLY: Tell them I'm upset.
ERICA: Will you shut up!

[CLARKE *turns. He is combing his hair.*]

CLARKE: [*To* ERICA] Oi!
ERICA: Yes. What is it now?
CLARKE: About time I came on.
ERICA: Is it?
CLARKE: Course it is. That's what the audience are waiting for. Wonderful me!
ERICA: [*To audience*] This is Clarke. The coolest dude in the school. Or so he thinks.
CLARKE: Oi! Wally!

[*He beckons to* WALLY, *as if he were calling a waiter.* WALLY *crosses to* CLARKE *SR.*]

CLARKE: Something up?

WALLY: Sadie doesn't love me.

CLARKE: You do surprise me.

WALLY: Why can't I be cool like you? What is it that I do wrong?

CLARKE: Well, for a start, you're the only boy in the school who wears flares.

WALLY: I like them. They give my legs room to breathe.

CLARKE: [*Pulling at* WALLY'*s anorak*] I mean—what is this?

WALLY: [*Zipping it up, proudly*] It's my anorak.

CLARKE: No-one wears an anorak nowadays!

WALLY: I do. It keeps me warm when I go bird-spotting.

CLARKE: Bird-spotting! You are such a prat!

WALLY: Why?

CLARKE: You don't understand the nineties, Wally. This is the age of toughness—Clint Eastwood, Dirty Den—Mrs Mangel. It's the age of image.

WALLY: Well you're tough, aren't you, Clarke? I mean—you wouldn't be scared of ending up behind the bicycle shed?

[*Cast sing dramatic chords.*]

CLARKE: [*Nervously*] What makes you say that?

WALLY: Well, isn't that what happens to people who borrow money off the Big Boss and don't pay it back? Blinking flip, I wouldn't like to do that, would you? I'd be in a right nervous state if I'd borrowed money off the Big Boss and couldn't pay it back. I mean I'd be really scared if I was . . .

CLARKE: Wally.

WALLY: Yes, Clarke.

CLARKE: Shut up.

ERICA: [*To audience*] See—the way I heard it, Clarke had borrowed a load of money to pay for the last tanker load of hair-gel he'd bought. He'd meant to pay it back of course, but the McDonald's where he worked had been closed down after someone found a bit of meat amongst all the plastic beefburger. And now he was getting a bit worried because the Big Boss was after him . . .

CLARKE: [*To* ERICA] Don't tell everyone that!

ERICA: Why not?

CLARKE: It's my image. Anyway it's not that bad, I'll find a way out . . .

[*A note is passed between the cast, eventually ending with* CLARKE. *He reads it and goes pale*.]

ERICA: What is it?

CLARKE: It's a piece of paper.

ERICA: What does it say?

CLARKE: The Big Boss wants to see me. Behind the bicycle sheds . . .

[*Cast sing dramatic chords.* CLARKE *and* WALLY *freeze*.]

ERICA: [*To audience*] I didn't hear no more about Clarke for the rest of the day. Anyway, what I say is this, if you're stupid enough to borrow money from the Big Boss, you've only got yourself to blame if you lose the use of your legs.

[*'Enter'* SADIE.]

ERICA: [*To* SADIE] You going to be busy tonight?

SADIE: I've got a modelling assignment.

ERICA: Really? What are you modelling?

[CLARKE *mimes being punched in the stomach*.]

ERICA: What did you say?

SADIE: I said I'm modelling . . .

[CLARKE*'s head snaps back as if kicked. He moans and falls to the ground*.]

ERICA: Look—it's Clarke!

[*They cross to where* CLARKE *lies SR.*]

SADIE: Clarke! Your hair's a mess!

CLARKE: I have been beaten up by several thugs. It's a bit difficult to keep your hair in place when someone's using your head as a punchbag.

ERICA: Ooooh. Is your nose broken?

CLARKE: Probably. I used it to block a punch.

ERICA: Shame. I always liked your nose.

CLARKE: So did I.

ERICA: The Big Boss's men did this to you.

CLARKE: You've got to help me. I've got to pay him back the money I owe him, or else he's going to beat me up properly.

ERICA: You mean this was just a practice run?

SADIE: You need medical attention.

CLARKE: You'll have to help me to a hospital.

SADIE: But Clarke! You're all dirty and bruised and covered in blood.

CLARKE: Oh silly me. Fancy bleeding!

SADIE: But I'm modelling tonight. If I help you I might get dirty or break a fingernail or something. I'm sorry, Clarke, I'd love to, really I would, but I can't. See you.

[*She crosses back to SL and freezes.*]

CLARKE: And I thought she was a friend. Come on then Erica . . .

ERICA: Look, it's like this Clarke. I just can't get involved.

CLARKE: But I need the money. And a bandage.

ERICA: But it's the Big Boss, Clarke! You know what happens if you get involved with him! You got yourself into this mess, you get yourself out of it. I'm a narrator—I can't afford to get involved with my characters.

CLARKE: Well thanks for all your help.

[*She returns to CS.* WALLY *starts peering around with his binoculars.* CLARKE *groans in agony.*]

WALLY: [*Looking through binoculars*] Did I hear the mating cry of a Greater Crested Grebe?

[CLARKE *moans again.*]

WALLY: Oh no, it's coming from this heap of rags in the corner.

CLARKE: It's me!

WALLY: Blinking flip! Clarke! Your hair's a mess.

CLARKE: Don't you start.

[WALLY *crosses to SR.*]

WALLY: What the heck happened to you?

CLARKE: I got beaten up, didn't I?

WALLY: Oooh. So you were in trouble, I thought so. I said to myself, 'He's in trouble if you ask me . . .'

CLARKE: Ohhhhh.

WALLY: Oh, silly me. Here, let me help you. You need to see matron.

[*He helps* CLARKE *to stand.*]

CLARKE: What's the point? She's only going to patch me up so that the Big Boss can beat me up again.

WALLY. Why is he going to beat you up again?

CLARKE: Because I still owe him the money.

WALLY: How much?

CLARKE: Fifty quid.

WALLY: Ooh crikey! Silly you. Well, never mind that, let's get you to matron. Don't you bleed a lot?

[CLARKE *turns and freezes.* WALLY *returns to CS and freezes. 'Enter'* ERICA.]

ERICA: [*To audience*] So anyway, it was later that evening when I found out what had happened. I was talking to Sadie . . .

SADIE: [*Interrupting*] Have you told them about me being a model yet?

ERICA: Of course I have, I told them on page one. Why can't you pay attention?

SADIE: I'm a bimbo. I don't have to pay attention. I just have to look sensuous.

ERICA: Yes, well, keep trying. And then in came Wally . . .

['*Enter*' WALLY.]

WALLY: Hello. [*To* SADIE] Hello light of my life.

SADIE: Ugggh! Look at you. You're all covered in blood. You look like you've been in a fight. Fancy walking around like that.

WALLY: Ah. Well, you see, I had to take someone to hospital.

ERICA: You got involved, eh?

WALLY: But you've got to help people haven't you? I mean that's being nice!

SADIE: Nice! What a wally.

['*Enter*' CLARKE, *combing his hair*.]

SADIE: Hello Clarke. Hair's looking better now.

ERICA: For the moment. Until the next time.

CLARKE: No, it's all right. Someone's paid it.

SADIE: Who?

CLARKE: No idea. I've just heard. Someone paid for me.

SADIE: Well, that's stupid.

CLARKE: Yeah—well, saved my bacon, that's all I'm worried about. Hi Wally.

[*He beckons* WALLY *across to him*.)

WALLY: Hello.

CLARKE: [*Pulling* WALLY *close and threatening him*] Listen, thanks for helping me and all that, but do us a favour eh? Don't tell anyone about it. I mean I got an image to protect and it don't do me any good for people to know that I got rescued by a bird-watcher in flares.

WALLY: [*Entirely without malice*] Oh—righty-ho Clarke.

['*Exit*' CLARKE and SADIE.]

ERICA: Wally, you paid that money didn't you?

WALLY: [*Coming CS*] Well—I happened to have it handy.

ERICA: I leave a character alone for a few minutes and you do something stupid. You're such a wally, Wally.

WALLY: Why?

ERICA: All this helping out! I mean—what do you hope to get out of it?

WALLY: Well . . . I don't know.

ERICA: You don't know. You help out someone who does nothing but take the mickey out of you, you give him the money to get him out of a hole he got himself in.

WALLY: It seemed like a nice thing to do.

ERICA: This is the nineties Wally. No-one cares what you do, only what you look like. When will you learn? Kindness is not cool.

WALLY: Oh.

ALL: Welcome to the nineties Wally.

WALLY: [*Waving*] Hello.

[*They freeze for a moment then exit.*]

Cluedo Hall

Characters:	Mr WADDINGTON—flamboyant. Miss SCARLET—Cockney. Mrs WHITE—maternal Northerner. Colonel MUSTARD—regimental, gruff. Rev. GREEN—Paisleyesque. Professor PLUM—dotty scientist. Mrs PEACOCK—well spoken, 'nice'. WADDINGTON JUNIOR—confident, assured.
Plot:	Parable of the tenants in the vineyard set in the world of the board-game, 'Cluedo'. The tenants refuse to pay their rent and kill the landlord's son in an effort to gain ownership of the hall.
Main Point:	Mankind does not give God his due and has rejected his Son, Jesus.
Running Time:	Approx 15 minutes.
Suitability:	Evangelistic event.
Staging:	All the characters stand in a semi-circle with their backs turned to the audience. At the appropriate time all they need to do is turn to face the audience. Those who 'die' need only turn round.

Props/Costumes: Each character can be dressed in their colour. WADDINGTON Senior and Junior need to be equally colourful in their attire—perhaps multicoloured. Weapons (rope, dagger, and lead piping) may be real or imaginary.

Remarks: Bear in mind that the WADDINGTONS are strong characters; confident, assertive and likeable. Too often, the God figure (Father or Son) comes across as a bit wet.

[*Miss* SCARLET *and Mrs* WHITE *DSR. Colonel* MUSTARD *and Rev* GREEN *CS. Prof* PLUM *and Mrs* PEACOCK *DSL. 'Enter' Mr* WADDINGTON. *He crosses from DSL to DSR during following speech.*]

WADDINGTON: Waddington's the name and fun's the game! In the beginning I created a universe of games. 'Let there be leisure!' I cried, and to the bored I gave the board! And it was good. On the second day I drew lines and divided spaces one from the other, and I named the spaces: Fenchurch Street, Mayfair, Piccadilly and Community Chest. Evening passed and morning came—that was the second day. On the third day I commanded, 'Let the spaces be filled', and so there were dice and property cards and bankers and battleships and little doggies and I saw that it was good. On the fourth day I said 'Let there be a hall that is vast and beautiful' and I named the hall 'Cluedo'. Then I said 'Let the hall be filled with ballrooms and conservatories, studies and libraries, with marble staircases, soft silk and exotic plants. On the sixth day I said, 'And now I will choose my tenants who will be responsible for the house, at the price of a modest rent and a contract to maintain the property in good order.' On the seventh day I rested. But now—look at my tenants . . .

['*Enter*' *Miss* SCARLET.]

SCARLET: Miss Scarlet, in the kitchen with me boyfriend—I mean with the boiler—and that's conked out—cut off by the electricity board, telephone disconnected and cooker reclaimed.

WADDINGTON: This tenant has brought my hall into moral disrepute and has refused to pay the rent.

SCARLET: I refuse to pay the rent.

[*Mr* WADDINGTON *observes (sitting or standing) from front edge of stage, DSR. 'Enter' Mrs* WHITE.]

WHITE: Well, it's no good me cooking the books. The head chef wants the dough, so pay up or beat it.

SCARLET: You don't understand, Mrs White. Me fifth husband 'asn't sent me alimony and me boyfriend's gone off with me meter money. Anyway, why should I pay for this doss 'ole? You should see the state of it after last night's party. There's glass on the grass, plates in the grates, mugs on the rugs. There's ash in the mash, drink in the sink and spew in the loo. There's bags, fags, mags, rags, rum, gum, crisp and crumb. There's brown ale, light ale, pale ale and stale ale. It's the truth—want more proof?

WHITE: Plead as long as you like Miss Harlot . . . er Scarlet. It's clear you've broken the rules of the game. Mr Waddington has given you a good starter and all the ingredients you need for a happy life. Pay up quick or you'll be out before you can say 'rotary mixer'.

SCARLET: Oh get stuffed you silly crab!

[*Miss* SCARLET *strangles Mrs* WHITE. *Both turn their backs on the audience.*]

WADDINGTON: Mrs White, in the kitchen with the rope. In the next room, the billiard room, lives Colonel Mustard.

[*'Enter' Colonel* MUSTARD, *muttering whilst cleaning his bayonet. 'Enter' Rev* GREEN.]

GREEN: [*Meekly*] Now—how shall I put it? Ah—I know. [*With venom, Paisley-like*] In that day those who have not paid their rent will be eternally damned, thrown into perpetual darkness, flung into fire and brimstone where there will be a screaming and a howling and a gnashing of teeth and repeats of 'Neighbours'. [*Sweetly*] Ding dong, parson calling!

MUSTARD: Who's that now? Pestilential rent collectors!

GREEN: [*Chanting*] I have been elected to bring the tithes into the storehouse, to gather the first fruits of the thanksgiving, the abundance of the harvest.

MUSTARD: What?

GREEN: I've come for the rent. Please.

MUSTARD: Pay Waddington? That state school pip-squeak! Needs to do some square bashing!

Thinks he owns the place—I didn't fight a war to pay rent.

GREEN: Well I don't quite . . .

MUSTARD: No time for detente. Surrender or bust!

GREEN: Well . . .

[*Colonel* MUSTARD *stabs him in the stomach. Both 'exit' by turning away from the audience.*]

WADDINGTON: Colonel Mustard in the billiard room with the dagger. And so, it was with a heavy heart that I sent the lovely Mrs Peacock to take my final warning to Professor Plum.

[*'Enter' Prof* PLUM, *conducting experiments.*]

PLUM: H_2sO_4 . . . NaC1 . . . $RpQz^5$ . . .

[*'Enter' Mrs* PEACOCK.]

PEACOCK: Morning Professor.

PLUM: Hold this.

PEACOCK: What's in it?

PLUM: Neutron bomb.

PEACOCK: But you could destroy the whole hall, Mr Waddington's beautiful creation!

PLUM: Shhh . . . Russians . . . sulphur solution . . . needs silence . . .

PEACOCK: Look here, Professor, this cannot go on. Not only are you destroying your room with sulphur burns and blowing out the bay windows, but you are jeopardising the whole hall with your toxic waste in the dustbins and acid rain clouds over the vegetable garden.

PLUM: Perfect safety precautions.

PEACOCK: I really must inform you . . .

[*Prof* PLUM *hits her on the head. They turn away.*]

WADDINGTON: Professor Plum in the conservatory with the lead piping. Well, when I saw how my tenants had treated my hall, how they'd dealt with my rent collectors, my heart broke. Why? Hadn't I made them, housed them, done all I could for them? They began to take the rules into their own hands, collected the dice and landed themselves in the ballroom.

[*Miss* SCARLET, *Prof* PLUM *and Colonel* MUSTARD *turn around and take one step DSC. There is a gathering discontent.*]

MUSTARD: Pestered by lower class rent collectors. Blood on the carpet.

PLUM: Interfering with our lives.

SCARLET: I've 'eard Waddington's sending 'is son. Do-gooder. Come to show us up with 'is ever-so-perfect life, I s'pose.

PLUM: You know what that means.

MUSTARD: Go to jail.

PLUM: Do not pass Go.

SCARLET: Do not collect £200.

MUSTARD: Can't do that.

PLUM: This place is ours—we've lived in it long enough.

SCARLET: Possession is nine tenths of the law.

[*Enter* WADDINGTON JUNIOR *SR.*]

PLUM: Who are you?

JUNIOR: I've come from my father—to sort out the contract and help clear up the mess.

MUSTARD: What mess? Nothing wrong with this place!

SCARLET: Do-gooder.

PLUM: You don't belong here. This is our hall.

JUNIOR: But you owe him everything. You're nothing without him. You must fulfil the contract.

SCARLET: 'Ow dare you suggest we're dependent on Waddington!

MUSTARD: We want the power.

PLUM: How do we know this Waddington exists?

SCARLET: We can cope.

MUSTARD,
PLUM,
SCARLET,
TOGETHER: We can cope. We can cope. We can cope.

[*All three approach* WADDINGTON JUNIOR, *taking hold of his arms and pinning him to an imaginary cross. Chant builds to a climax and then freeze.*]

WADDINGTON: Jesus Christ. On earth. With nails.

[*Exit.*]

The Invitation

by Roger Porthouse

Characters:	Old MAN
	BOY—a teenager.
	GIRL—a teenager.
	VOICE—voice offstage.
Plot:	Boy meets girl. Well . . . almost.
Main Point:	Don't procrastinate!
Running Time:	Approx 10 minutes.
Suitability:	Evangelistic event.
Staging:	Bench, or row of chairs to seat three.
Props/Costumes:	Cane and newspaper for MAN Deodorant and notes for BOY. Mirror and watch for GIRL.

[MAN *is sitting on park bench doing a crossword puzzle. Enter* BOY *at a run. Looks round. Sits SL of* MAN*, still looking round. Enter* GIRL *at a run. Sees* BOY*, stops, checks her dress, then walks DSR.* BOY *sees* GIRL.]

BOY: It's her!

[MAN *looks to* BOY*, thinking he is talking to him. Realises he isn't, so listens to both* BOY *and* GIRL *as passive spectator whilst completing crossword.*]

BOY: A little late, but she's here! Right, keep calm. [*Fidgeting*] She's just another girl . . . whom I happen to fancy.
[*Tries various sitting positions.*]

GIRL: Okay, my little friend, here goes. It's your last chance, so don't muck it up! I hope he can see me . . .

BOY: [*Finding most impressive position, arms behind head*] There! That's it—be casual, be calm. [*Sniffs armpits, panics*] Phew! I *knew* I'd forget something. [*Drops arms to side*]

GIRL: [*Breathing deeply*] Mmmm, my favourite aftershave.
[*There is barking offstage.* GIRL *looks.*]

BOY: Right. Now, here's your chance, sunshine.
[*He gets deodorant out and sprays under arms, over his clothes.* GIRL *looks round.* BOY *throws spray over his shoulder as he smiles at* GIRL. *She quickly turns forward again.*]

GIRL: He smiled at me.

BOY: She smiled at me!

GIRL: [*Romantic*] It's love!

BOY: [*Eager*] Session on!
[MAN *gives up crossword to concentrate on* BOY *and* GIRL.]

GIRL: Oh, I do wish he'd make his move. What on earth is he doing?
[*She gets out her mirror to spy on him.*]

BOY: She's got her mirror out . . . perhaps she's waiting for someone else? No—stay cool, Phil. Get a grip on yourself. [*Grabbing* MAN's *arm*] Stop panicking and take your time. [*Realises he is holding* MAN's *arm*] Oh, sorry.

GIRL: [*Impatient*] Come on, come on. I haven't got long, as it is. It's typical, isn't it? He finally raises the effort to smile at me and it's the day

I'm leaving town! I haven't overdone it on the make-up have I? [*She checks*]

BOY: Boy, she looks good. You've got to ask her today, Phil! It's been six months now. Six months! Same park, same bench, same time, same day ... what are you, man or mouse? [*He thinks hard about this one*] Mouse. I'll ask her next week. Oh no! No! You said that last week and the week before that. [*Thinks*] And the week before that, come to think of it.

GIRL: He's got seven minutes and that's it. No more unspoken hello's, no more chances, just two broken hearts ... well ... [*sad*] one, anyway.

BOY: Right, get up and go for it!

[*He stands up and looks straight at* GIRL.]

GIRL: [*Excited*] He's up! Six months and he's finally got up! He's *got* to ask me now.

BOY: [*Cowardly despair*] No, I can't! [*He sits*]

GIRL: [*Cold, emotionless*] He's down.

BOY: No, I've got to! Get up! [*Stands*] Keep your distance, Phil.

[*Moves DSL.*]

GIRL: He's up again, he's up. Move away, girl, don't look at him.

BOY: Hang on, what am I meant to do now?

GIRL: [*Thinking fast*] Tactics, girl, tactics. Play hard to get. You don't want him to think you're a slag.

BOY: [*Finding note in pocket*] Oh yeah—the chat up line. [*Reading slowly and without expression*] Hi—my—name—is—state name—what's—yours? Eh? Oh, silly me. Hi—my—name—is—Phil—what's—yours? [*Cool, with feeling*] Hi, my name's Phil. What's yours?

GIRL: But don't play *too* hard to get, otherwise you might lose him.

BOY: No, not catchy enough. [*Searches pockets for other notes*]

GIRL: He must know I like him, I haven't spoken to him in six months.

BOY: Ah—here we go. [*Reads*] Hi, I'm Phil. How about some oscular therapy?

GIRL: I mean, what does he want? A sign round my neck saying 'take me'? Actually . . . no, no, you can't! [*Checks time*] Four minutes.

BOY: Nope. A touch too clinical. Hang on, will she be looking at my best side? [*Tries to find best profile*] Hi—do you want to learn some great new tongue twisters?

GIRL: Ooh, I've got butterflies in my stomach.

BOY: Impress her, that's it! Would you like the keys to my Triumph Herald?

GIRL: [*Romantic*] Perhaps if I fainted he would dive to my rescue and give me the kiss of life?

BOY: It's no good, Phil. You're just going to have to let the words flow naturally. There's no backing down now. Get ready.

GIRL: [*Checking time again*] Oh my word! Three minutes! I'm going to have to try it. Brace yourself!

BOY: [*Building up courage*] Set . . .

GIRL: [*About to faint*] Here goes . . .

BOY: Go! [*Rapidly to* GIRL] Hello.

GIRL: [*Just beginning to fall, stopping herself*] Argh! . . . Hi!

BOY: I did it! I said hello!

GIRL: [*Shocked*] He said hello! And I answered him!

BOY: Hope she doesn't think I'm too forward.

GIRL: [*Keen*] Say it again. Say it again!

BOY: [*Proud*] But you said it, Phil. You said hello. Oh, you stud, you!

GIRL: [*Hurried*] Two and a half minutes.

BOY: [*Still gloating*] Think of it! 'Oh look! There goes Phil "The Stud" Johnstone' ... oh dammit, I was too forward!

GIRL: [*Impatient, flat*] I feel like a stuffed prune standing here. Two minutes.

BOY: No, no, calm down, Phil. You're on target.

GIRL: Why won't he talk to me? Oh, I wish he'd have another go.

BOY: You've made contact.

GIRL Minute and a half ...

BOY: And the line's open. What now? [*Thinks*] Got it!
[BOY *takes a side step towards* GIRL.]

GIRL: That's the idea! Right. Respond girl, respond.
[GIRL *takes a step closer.*]

BOY: It's working! Phil Johnstone, armed with net and grappling hook goes to find himself a woman ...

GIRL: [*Sniggering*] I'll have to buy a new leash. Forty five seconds.
[BOY *and* GIRL *step closer at the same time.*]

BOY: She stepped closer at the same time. She wants me. Time for a bit of fun.
[BOY *turns away.*]

GIRL: Oh no! Not now, you idiot!

BOY: That'll get her going!

GIRL: [*Panic*] Twenty seconds!
[GIRL *now facing* BOY *steps closer.* BOY *faces DS.*]

BOY: Right now, be cool, be calm, be casual.
[BOY *takes hasty step nearer.* BOY *and* GIRL *now almost side by side.*]

GIRL: Fifteen seconds ... There's hardly enough time left to exchange phone numbers ...

BOY: Right Phil, usual rules. Countdown from ten to zero. On the count of zero, you *have* to ask her out. Otherwise you're a sissy.

GIRL: [*Despair*] Ten seconds left.

BOY: Right then, when you're ready. [*Sniggers*] And ten . . .

GIRL: Nine.

BOY: And nine . . .

GIRL: Eight—oh hurry up! [*She checks over her shoulder*]

BOY: [*Finding it a strain*] Eight.

GIRL: Seven seconds and that's it.

BOY: Seven. Lucky seven.

GIRL: Six.

BOY: Six.

GIRL: [*Backing away slowly*] If I weren't leaving, I'd come back next week.

BOY: Five . . . oh, did I say six? Yeah. Five.

VOICE: [*Offstage, distant*] Jessica . . . ?

GIRL: [*Still backing away*] Oh no!

BOY: Four.

GIRL: Farewell, silent friend.

BOY: [*Concentrating on counting*] Three.

[GIRL *backs further away.*]

BOY: Two. Come on Phil, you've got to do it.

GIRL: It could have been fun.

VOICE: Jessica?

BOY: One . . .

[GIRL *blows a kiss and runs off.*]

BOY: [*Turning*] Look, I was wondering if you'd like to come out . . . [*he notices that* GIRL *is no longer there*] . . . for . . . a . . . drink . . . sometime. [*Pause*] I'll, ah, see you next week then? Same time, same bench, same park. S-so. I'll be here. [*Pause*] Oh well, plenty more fish in the sea.

[BOY *stands there for a moment, looks at* MAN, *shrugs and exits SL.*]

MAN: [*Getting up slowly*] Ah, funny. [*Shakes head woefully*] That's exactly what I said.

[*He picks up his cane and paper and hobbles offstage.*]

'To Boldly Go . . .'

Characters:	BURK—Captain of the Starship. SOCK—Vulcan First Officer. YOOHOO—Communications Officer. PUNK, BAG LADY, MAN } Victims.
Plot:	'Star Trek' spoof in which the crew 'beam down' to evangelise the neighbourhood.
Main Point:	Evangelism is not something that can be reduced to a particular method or technique. Nor is it always easy.
Running Time:	7 minutes.
Suitability:	Church event.
Staging:	Chair for BURK. Chair for YOOHOO.
Props/Costumes:	'Star Trek' badges. Pointed ears for SOCK. Personal hi-fi. Matchboxes to represent scanners and radios. Glitter/pieces of foil to represent 'beaming down'. Plastic bags for the BAG LADY.
Remarks:	The more references you can get to the original, the better. Many joke shops sell Spock ears, or inflatable 'Starship Enterprises'. 'Beaming down' can be mimicked by the person

singing a high-pitched 'Ooo' and throwing a handful of glitter and torn up silver foil into the air above him/her.

[*Enter the Crew. They adopt positions on stage roughly similar to the bridge of the Enterprise.* BURK *sits stage centre.* SOCK *stands USL, looking into his sensor.* YOOHOO *sits USR, holding her earpiece to her ear.*]

BURK: Space—the final frontier. These are the voyages of the Starship St Kevin and All Saints, their five week mission to evangelise the neighbourhood, to make new converts, to boldly go where no church has gone before!
[*The crew sing the* STAR TREK *theme. Someone rushes across stage holding an inflatable Starship Enterprise.*]

BURK: Vicar's log, stardate 26/3/88.2. That's 071 if you're outside London. We are orbiting the local area in an attempt to make contact. What's the sensor reading Mr Sock?

SOCK: It's a shapeless, ugly landscape, Captain. Sensors indicate a complete absence of intelligent life. It's the shopping centre.

BURK: Right. Yoohoo—are you ready?

YOOHOO: Yes Captain, I'm really keen. And my programme of events is ready.

BURK: This should get 'em in.

YOOHOO: Beam me down Mr Sock.
[*She beams down SR. She stands next to a* PUNK, *who is wearing a personal hi-fi.*]

YOOHOO: Er . . . hello.
[*The* PUNK *ignores her.*]

YOOHOO: I . . . I was wondering if you'd like to . . .

PUNK: What?

YOOHOO: Could you turn the music down a bit?

PUNK: What?

YOOHOO: [*Shouting*] I said could you turn down the music a bit!

PUNK: All right—no need to yell.

YOOHOO: Oh, I was wondering if you'd care to come to our young people's fellowship? It's very good. We play the guitars, and sing, and . . . er . . . play the guitars again. And there's squash and biscuits.

[The PUNK *puts her headphones on again and walks off SR.*]

YOOHOO: [*Shouting after her*] We've an outreach concert on the fourteenth. It's a folksinger and a lady missionary from Nepal. Oh . . . er . . . [*into the radio*] beam me up, Mr Sock.

[*She is beamed back into the ship, and collapses into her seat.*]

BURK: Was it bad, Yoohoo?

YOOHOO: The apathy, Captain! She wasn't interested in the concert or the youth fellowship or anything!

BURK: Well—you tried anyway. Mr Sock, it's your turn now. Are you ready?

SOCK: Of course, Captain. All we have to do is approach the situation logically. I have here the results of my surveys, my carefully planned evangelism method, my charts, information pack, person to person video, Billy Graham Mission '89 wig. Everything I need.

BURK: Right then, what's our position?

SOCK: Well, you're sitting down, I'm standing next to you, Chekhov's in the bath . . .

BURK: Where are we?

SOCK: Sensors indicate a derelict wasteland, covered with a thin layer of animal refuse. It's the park.

BURK: Beam down, Mr Sock.

SOCK: At once, Captain.

[SOCK *beams down. He arrives next to a* BAG WOMAN *SL.*]

WOMAN: Oooh!

SOCK: [*Using scanners*] Scanner indicates a humanoid female of advanced years. Logically, this presents no problem. I will simply use approach 5(*b*). The 'speak very loudly and assume all old people are stupid' approach. [*To* WOMAN] Hello dear! Hello! How are you then? What about this weather we're having then? Bitter isn't it? How would you like a nice cup of tea then? Down the church—a nice cup of tea and a game of bingo! You come with me then . . .

[SOCK *takes her by the arm.*]

WOMAN: You take your hands off me, you pervert!

SOCK: Excuse me, but this approach was demographically designed to cater for your age and social status.

WOMAN: Get off!

[*She starts hitting him with her umbrella or bag.* SOCK *uses the Vulcan 'grip' on her and she stands there paralysed. He turns away, smiles knowingly and takes out his radio. She comes out of the paralysis and starts hitting him again.*]

SOCK: Er . . . beam me up Captain . . . quick!

[*He is beamed back to the ship.* WOMAN *exits SL.*]

BURK: Vicar's log. Stardate 65/35/85. Mr Sock's logical, planned approach has failed as swiftly as Yoohoo's keenness. There's only one thing for it, I must go down there myself.

SOCK: Captain, it's dangerous down there. I must advise you not to go.

BURK: Thanks for your concern, Sock.

SOCK: Concern? That is a human emotion Captain. I am merely thinking logically. You're the only one with the key to the executive toilet.

BURK: Sock—I've got to go.

SOCK: My feelings exactly, Captain.

YOOHOO: Captain! What are you going to do?

BURK: We've tried to lure them in. We've tried the logical approach. It's time to get tough!

YOOHOO: But Captain! It's hell down there!

BURK: I know. That's why I'm going.

[*He is beamed down to find himself in a pub SR. A* MAN *is propped against the bar, drinking.* BURK *approaches him.*]

BURK: All right. How do you stand with the Lord?

MAN: What?

BURK: Are you washed in the blood of the Lamb? Where would you go if you died tonight?

MAN: Are you threatening me?

BURK: Repent, for you are an evil sinner. We have all sinned! But you especially.

MAN: Look, I'm just having a quiet drink, see? And you're interfering, right? So unless you want a mouthful of signet rings I suggest you shut it.

BURK: But it's for your own good.

MAN: I'm going to count to five and if you're not out of this pub you'll find yourself picking up your teeth from the car park. One . . .

[MAN *proceeds to count.*]

BURK: [*Into radio*] Beam me up. What do you mean you can't. I don't care if the line's engaged! Beam me up before I get . . .

[*He is beamed up.* MAN *exits SL.*]

BURK: Pulverised. Ahem. Well—he certainly wasn't very open to the gospel.

YOOHOO: Are you all right, Captain?

BURK: I think we may have to revise our plans a bit.

YOOHOO: Yes, I mean—are they the type we really want on board ship?

SOCK: I think we need to spend a bit more time preparing, Captain. I'll draw up some more statistics.

YOOHOO: I'll plan another outreach evening.

BURK: I'll read another tract.

ALL: And we'll all stay in space, where it's safe!

[*They give the Vulcan finger 'greeting' and freeze. Then exit.*]

LESSON THREE
LONGER SKETCHES

It is only within the framework of the longer theatrical pieces that one can fully get to grips with a character. After all, *Hamlet* is two-and-a-half hours long. I don't think it would have worked half as well as a ten-minute piece for church services. Oh I don't know though . . .

I remember the longest piece I ever played in was one of Peter Brook's masterpieces—a theatrical version of the Oxford English Dictionary. I played volume three: 'CA—DE'. The performance lasted twenty-seven days and the audience had to be kept awake by drugs and by periodically hitting them with hammers.

Anyway, the point is this: there's a lot more to remember, so rule number one—*Remember the lines* – is very important here.

Pace is also important. Longer pieces can drag a little, so try and gabble as much as you can. It's amazing the time you can save by really rushing your words. We did *Man and Superman* in six minutes once. Never mind if the audience can't hear you, they'll just assume it's some kind of abstract theatre.

Eddie

Characters: EDDIE—nervous and insecure schoolboy.
MOTHER—generally ignores him.
FATHER—a man of many parts.
DRIPPER—the neanderthal school bully.
MIRANDA—incurable romantic.
TEACHER
CHEMIST
ANNOUNCER—in advert.

Plot: EDDIE is all things to all men. Plagued by spots, the school bully and parents who think he is a genius, he finally reaches a point where he prays and really experiences Jesus. After that he stands up for his faith. He still gets hit, though.

Main Point: That we all need a *real* experience of God. That our faith has to be based on something solid.

Running Time: 20 minutes.

Suitability: Evangelistic, church, you name it . . .

Staging: SR has 3 chairs set out in a line facing SL, like a schoolroom. Unsurprisingly, it's the school. SL has two chairs placed facing the audience representing EDDIE's home. The action moves between these places, other action taking place SC.

Props/Costumes: Zitblast and mirror for advert. Book for MIRANDA. Essays for TEACHER. Briefcase for FATHER. Everything else can be mimed.

Remarks: This is a very versatile piece, but it needs plenty of 'pace'. All the action needs to be slick as you rely a lot on mime and the audience's imagination.

[*Enter the cast who stand SC to do the advert. They should remain immobile until they speak. The jingle can be spoken or sung to a simple tune.*]

ANNOUNCER: [*With menace*] When you're alone in the dark, there's no need to be afraid of ghosts, or ghouls, or spots that go bump in the night!

GIRL: [*Holds mirror to her face. Screams*] Oh no! I need Zitblast!

[*She holds up a box marked 'Zitblast' and grins a sickly grin.*]

JINGLE: If you have spots or pimples,
No need to stay so blemished,
Just get a tube of Zitblast
From your local chemist.

[*Exit cast, leaving* EDDIE *SC. He yawns and stretches his arms.*]

MOTHER: [*From offstage*] Wake up, Eddie! Time for church!

EDDIE: [*To audience, waking up*] That's Mum. She and Dad like me to go to church. They think that personal religious beliefs are very important. That's why they stay in bed and meditate on Sunday mornings. [*He mimes washing his face and finds a spot*] Oh noooo! Look at the size of that zit! Looks like Mount Vesuvius. [*He bursts it*] What was that advert I saw last night? Zitblast! I'll go and get some.

[*Enter* CHEMIST *SL and* CUSTOMERS *SR. They cross to SC and look round the shop.* EDDIE *enters the Chemist's.*]

CHEMIST: Yes, sonny, can I help you?

EDDIE: [*Self-conscious*] Er ... don't you want to serve these other people first?

CHEMIST: No, I think they're all right. You're all right aren't you?

CUSTOMERS: [*Looking around them*] Yes, yes fine.

CHEMIST: See? They're waiting for prescriptions. Now what can I do for you?

EDDIE: [*Whispering*] I'd like some Zitblast please.

CHEMIST: What?

EDDIE: Zitblast!

CHEMIST: [*Loudly*] Oh Zitblast!

EDDIE: Shhhhh!!

[*The other customers look at* EDDIE.]

CHEMIST: I'll have a look. No, no, we've not got any out. I'll see if there's any in stock.

EDDIE: Right.

CHEMIST: [*Shouting offstage*] Fred! There's a young lad out here wants some Zitblast for his spots. What? [*Looks at Eddie*] Oh—he'll need extra large I reckon.

[*In a fit of embarrassment,* EDDIE *runs out of the shop. The* CHEMIST *and* CUSTOMERS *form a congregation standing in line SC and singing a hymn.* EDDIE *squeezes among them.*]

EDDIE: [*To audience*] See what I mean? Life conspires against me. I suppose I'm insecure. Maybe that's why I like church. I enjoy it at church and I believe it, really I do. But it all seems to fade away at school on Monday mornings.

[*Exit church congregation variously. Enter* MIRANDA *and* DRIPPER *SR.*]

EDDIE: [*To audience*] This is my school—St Kevin's Comprehensive for the oppressed working class. And that's Dripper. He's the official school bully. He's very good at it—he's won cups for assault and battery and he injures people for the county youth side.

[MIRANDA *sits on L-hand chair and* DRIPPER *on R-hand chair.* EDDIE *moves across to school, and stands by where* MIRANDA *is sitting.*]

EDDIE: [*To audience*] That's Miranda. She's all right, but a bit . . . well, romantic, if you know what I mean. I quite like her really.

[DRIPPER, *in the seat behind, gobs on the centre chair, just as* EDDIE *sits down. He starts to react, but the* TEACHER *enters SL.*]

TEACHER: All right, settle down, settle down. I have here your homework, for what it's worth. The subject, if you cast your grubby little minds back, was the octopus.

[*She hands the homework out.*]

TEACHER: Miranda, yours was interesting. But I think you ought to know that when I set an essay I expect an essay in return, not a forty-eight page epic poem beginning, 'I wandered lonely as an octopus'. Eddie, yours was excellent. Plenty of facts, succinct argument, impressive reasoning. The one, tiny fault I found was that you had copied it entirely from 'The Encyclopaedia Britannica'. Nice try.

[*She examines* DRIPPER*'s contribution which is on a miniscule piece of paper.*]

TEACHER: Dripper! Dripper, you excelled yourself. [*Reads*] 'The Octopus' by Dripper. 'The octopus is an eight sided cat.' Well down to your usual standard. You might have drawn a picture or something.

DRIPPER: I ain't got no pencil.

TEACHER: [*Correcting his grammar*] I *have* no pencil. He or she *has* no pencils. They *have* no pencils.

DRIPPER: [*Pause*] Well, who's got all the pencils then?

[*He starts to pick his nose.*]

TEACHER: Don't pick your nose boy, your head will cave in.

[DRIPPER *obedient to the last, wipes his hand on* EDDIE*'s back.*]

TEACHER: Open your textbooks 'Horrible things to do to frogs' Volume one. Page eighty-six. Get on with your dissection.

[*She exits SL.*]

DRIPPER: Oi Smiff!

EDDIE: [*Nervous*] Who, me?

DRIPPER: Yeah, you.

EDDIE: What can I do for you?

DRIPPER: I 'eard you were coming out of church yesterday.

EDDIE: Who me? Never!

DRIPPER: I don't like religious nutters, see?

EDDIE: [*Panicking*] No, no, no, can't have been me Dripper 'cos I don't believe a word of it, I've never believed a word of it and please don't hit me.

DRIPPER: Right. Just as long as we know how we stand.

EDDIE: [*To audience.*] Phew! It's survival of the fittest see. As this frog is about to find out, life is all about power.

[EDDIE *stabs at frog.* DRIPPER *and* MIRANDA *exit SR.* EDDIE *crosses to home. Enter* MOTHER *SL. She sits and knits, looking vacantly at the TV.*]

EDDIE: I'm home!

MOTHER: Hello dear. Did you have a good day at school?

EDDIE: Not bad. The headmaster caught fire. Then an earthquake wrecked the gymnasium, Miss Clutterbuck, the maths teacher, ran amok with an axe, the Martians invaded and you're not listening to a word I'm saying are you?

MOTHER: Yes, dear—you were talking rubbish. You always do when you get home from school. Now get on with your homework.

EDDIE: [*To audience*] My parents have somehow got it into their heads that I'm a genius and they keep expecting me to prove them right. I have to hide all my marks and disguise all my reports.

[*There is a sound of coughing offstage.*]

MOTHER: Oh—here's your Father back.

[FATHER *enters SL.*]

FATHER: Eh up, lad! Eh, but it were hard work down t'pit today. Forty ton we must have shifted wi' nowt but a pick and shovel.

[*He coughs badly.*]

FATHER: Eh but the coal dust gets up t'lungs summut rotten!

EDDIE: [*Pause*] I don't know why you come in each night and complain about conditions down the mine. You're an accountant.

FATHER: Oh. Oh yes. Keep forgetting.

[*Exit* FATHER *SL.*]

EDDIE: Mum, why does Dad keep pretending to be a miner?

MOTHER: Well, it's not easy for him being an accountant. He doesn't like to own up to it.

EDDIE: Yeah, but he's getting worse.

MOTHER: Dinner!

[*She exits SL to get dinner.* EDDIE *sits down.*]

FATHER: [*Entering SL*] Dinner! Yum yum. Sorry about all that earlier son, about being a coal miner. Don't know what came over me.

[*He sits on L-hand chair, next to* EDDIE.]

FATHER: I should face facts, shouldn't I? Get used to the idea that I'm just a plain, boring, run of the mill brain surgeon!

EDDIE: Accountant.

FATHER: Accountant! That's what I mean.

MOTHER: [*Enters from SL, bringing on food*] Had any good marks recently?

EDDIE: Well, Miss Trendpot, the biology teacher, said my biology essay was excellent.

MOTHER: Hear that, Father? Excellent!

FATHER: What else did she say?

EDDIE: Er . . . she said it had plenty of facts, impressive arguments and succinct reasoning.

MOTHER: Oh, Eddie, you're going to be something special. We're so proud of you!

[MOTHER *and* FATHER *freeze.* EDDIE *stands and moves SC.*]

EDDIE: [*To audience*] You see—my life's a mess. I'm a Christian at church, an atheist at school and a genius at home. And there doesn't seem to be any way out.

[*Exit* MOTHER *and* FATHER *SL.* EDDIE *turns away from the audience.*]

MOTHER: [*Offstage*] Wake up Eddie! Time for school!

EDDIE: [*Turning, yawning and waking up*] Ah well—another day. [*Mimes washing and looking in the mirror, and discovers another spot.*] Oh good grief! Not another one! I can't do any more. I'm already the cleanest person in the world. I even wash the soap before I use it. School again! Roll on lunchtime!

[*Crosses to SR and enters canteen, holding tray. Enter* MIRANDA *SR. She sits and mimes eating. She is reading her book.*]

EDDIE: Is anyone sitting here?

MIRANDA: Not unless he's the invisible man, no.

EDDIE: Ah [*Gives incredibly false laugh*] Invisible man, joke, like it. Your book good?

MIRANDA: Wonderful—it's so romantic.

EDDIE: What's it called?

MIRANDA: 'Doctor never does'. It's all about this nurse, only she's only become a nurse because her husband was killed in the war, and she falls in love with this doctor—tall, handsome, Rock Enzyme—and then her husband turns up again as one of her patients. It's terribly romantic!

EDDIE: Yeah terrible . . . terribly romantic.

MIRANDA: [*Leaping up from her seat and reading with passion*] Take me away from all this! I can't stand it any more!

EDDIE: Er . . . is your lunch all right?

MIRANDA: I was reading from the book.

EDDIE: Oh, the book.

MIRANDA: [*Sitting and continuing to read*] She opened the door in her flimsy frock and there stood the tall, brooding figure of Rock Enzyme.

'Oh Rock . . .' she gasped, 'It's you!'
'I had to come,' he said in his deep, butch voice. 'Did I startle you? I know it's late but, you see I want to marry you!'
'Oh Rock,' Sylvia gasped. 'I can't join you in wedlock, Doc. I don't care about the frock or the clock or the shock of the knock, Rock, but I've news from Bangkok! My husband's bock' . . . er . . . back. How romantic! Doesn't that send thrills of excitement through you?

EDDIE: Are you going to eat your pudding? 'Cos if you're not I'll have it.

MIRANDA: You're ignorant, you are. You don't care anything about fine art. You're nothing but a Palestine.

EDDIE: No—I think the word is Philistine.

MIRANDA: Is it?

EDDIE: I think so. They're in the Bible. They're in One Samuel, Two Samuel . . . er Son of Samuel, Samuel Strikes Back, they're in that lot . . .

MIRANDA: You read the Bible?

EDDIE: I do a bit, yeah.

MIRANDA: I didn't know you were religious, Eddie. I've always wanted to meet someone deeply spiritual.
[*She puts her hand on his knee.*]

EDDIE: [*Pause*] Oh I'm deep. I am really deep. I'm bottomless. In a manner of speaking.

MIRANDA: How thrilling!

EDDIE: Amen!

MIRANDA: What?

EDDIE: Just, you know, praying.

MIRANDA: Oh Eddie! I never knew you were so holy. You're almost a saint, really, aren't you?

EDDIE: Yeah, it's just a formality really. Listen, there's a film on tonight at the Roxy—'Indiana Jones and the Lavatory of Doom'. You wouldn't like to come and see it?

MIRANDA: Oh Eddie! I couldn't! I couldn't!

EDDIE: Why not?

MIRANDA: I couldn't be so selfish as to drag you away from your devotions.

EDDIE: Oh no—you wouldn't because us saints, we get through them really quickly . . .

MIRANDA: No. A holy man like you shouldn't be driven to sin by a beautiful temptress like me. I'll go and leave you to contemplate.

EDDIE: No—I'm not that holy!

[*She exits SR.*]

EDDIE: [*Shouting after her*] I mean—what's a bit of temptation between friends? Oh rats!

[*Goes home. Enter* MOTHER *SL.*]

MOTHER: Hello dear. Did you have a good day at school?

EDDIE: Why do you always say that?

MOTHER: Say what?

EDDIE: [*Mimicking her*] Hello dear. Did you have a good day at school?

MOTHER: Well, what would you like me to say?

EDDIE: I don't know. Say something different. *Do* something different. Do something you've never done before. Cook a nice meal or something.

MOTHER: Oh you're just being temperamental. Geniuses are temperamental, or so I've heard.

EDDIE: Mum, this genius business . . .

[*His confession is interrupted by* FATHER *who hops onto stage SL, doing his Long John Silver impression, whilst holding a briefcase.*]

FATHER: Ah-harr, Jim lad! We've been cruising down the Spanish main, curse me gizzards and stap me vitals! Ah-harr!

EDDIE: Hello Father, had a good day at the office? Done lots of adding up?

FATHER: [*Embarrassedly putting his leg down*] Ahem. I'm going to get changed.
[*Exits SL.*]

EDDIE: We've got to do something about him, he's getting worse.

MOTHER: He wants to impress you. He wants you to be proud of him.

EDDIE: How can I be proud of him? He's a complete nutter!

MOTHER: Don't say that! He's your Father! He deserves a little respect. I never want to hear you say that again.
[*Re-enter* FATHER *SL.*]

FATHER: [*German accent*] Oh I'm vorn out! It takes it out of you, splitting ze atom.
[*He sits down.*]

MOTHER: You're right—he is a nutter. [*Shouting in his ear*] Pull yourself together, Father!

FATHER: Atom? Did I say atom? I meant accounts.

EDDIE: You don't have to try and impress me, Dad. I don't care what you do.

FATHER: But son, you don't understand. I don't want you to end up like I have! I don't want you to be an accountant . . .

MOTHER: It's all right, Father, don't you worry. Our boy's clever, aren't you Eddie?

EDDIE: No I'm not! I'm not clever or intelligent or anything!

MOTHER: Is something wrong dear?

EDDIE: Look—I . . . I'm not the cross between Einstein and Daley Thompson you think I am.

FATHER: But son—your marks!

EDDIE: Lies. Porkies! I'm all right, average, nothing special.

MOTHER: But if you work hard!

EDDIE: Oh—you're not listening!

[He crosses to SC. Exit MOTHER *and* FATHER *SL.]*

EDDIE: *[To audience]* I went out, slamming the door behind me for good measure. Outside it was a typical English summer's evening and the rain was lovely and warm. I just wanted to walk, to be alone. It was funny, the church door was open and almost without thinking about it, I went in. I just wanted to have something real, something I could trust. I just wanted a friend. Suddenly I found myself praying, I mean *really* praying, not just mouthing the words, and it was as if someone was there. It was as if someone I'd heard about, and read about, but never met, had come in and put his arm around me! I rushed out of church and rushed home, burst in through the front door and said, 'Mum, Dad, something's happened!' But they weren't there, they'd gone to bed. I didn't half feel stupid.

[Enter DRIPPER *SR.]*

DRIPPER: Oi, Smith!

EDDIE: Who me?

DRIPPER: Yeah, you.

[He beckons to EDDIE *who comes towards him. They stand, facing each other SC.]*

EDDIE: *[Nervous]* What can I do for you, Dripper?

DRIPPER: I heard, right, that you was seen coming out of church again!

EDDIE: Ah.

DRIPPER: Proper little choirboy, aren't we?

EDDIE: [*Timidly*] Yeah, well, I was praying.

DRIPPER: Oh, praying is it? Well, you remember what I said last time?

EDDIE: [*Very timidly*] Yeah—but I was still praying.

DRIPPER: You little goody-goody!

EDDIE: [*Losing temper*] Oh, stick it up your nose, you great fat barrel of lard!

[*There is a pause.* EDDIE *realises what he's done.*]

EDDIE: Aaaaaahhh!

[*He holds his head in his hands.*]

DRIPPER: What?

EDDIE: Now, now Dripper, let's talk about this. There is more to life than grievous bodily harm, you know. You can't go through life burying your head in your Enid Blyton books!

DRIPPER: No-one talks to Dripper like that. Nobody insults Noddy!

[*He hits Eddie, and then knees him in a certain place. They freeze in that pose. Enter* ANNOUNCER *SL.*]

ANNOUNCER: There are two things to remember about bullies. One is that they are insecure, lonely creatures. The other is that they are violent and extremely dangerous. We should like to point out that we are all trained actors and have spent many years perfecting this dangerous stunt. Please do not try it at home. Thank you.

[ANNOUNCER *exits SL. The action recommences.*]

DRIPPER: And this is for Noddy!

[*He head-butts* EDDIE *and exits SL.* EDDIE *falls to the ground and* MIRANDA *enters SR.*]

MIRANDA: Eddie! What happened to you?

EDDIE: I hit Dripper in the fist with my eye. Then I groined him in the knee.

[*She helps him to a seat SR.*]

MIRANDA: You've been fighting!

EDDIE: I have not. He was fighting, I was rolling around in agony.

MIRANDA: Let me look—oh you're wounded!

EDDIE: [*Taking the opportunity*] Am I? Oh, yes—I think I am. [*Putting it on*] Ooooh the pain!

MIRANDA: Here let me soothe you.

[*She lays his head in her lap and strokes it. His head, that is, not her lap. Pay attention.*]

MIRANDA: Does it hurt?

EDDIE: Agony! Keep stroking.

MIRANDA: Fancy beating you up! You—a man of God.

EDDIE: Ah—yes, I've got a confession to make about that!

MIRANDA: A confession! I didn't realise it was that bad. I'll fetch a priest.

[*She leaps up, depositing* EDDIE *on the floor.*]

EDDIE: [*Getting up and dusting himself down*] No, no, not that sort of confession. All that religious bit, I was putting it on.

MIRANDA: You mean you're not a saint?

EDDIE: I'm afraid not. But I do believe, really. That's why Dripper hit me. I was telling him about church, I was telling him I prayed.

MIRANDA: I see.

EDDIE: And I called him a great fat barrel of lard.

[*Enter* DRIPPER *SL.*]

DRIPPER: [*Seeing* MIRANDA *and* EDDIE]What 'ave we here then—the wounded soldier?

EDDIE: Ignore him.

DRIPPER: Learned your lesson then?

EDDIE: Go away. I haven't got anything left to bruise.

MIRANDA: Yeah—go away, you great fat horrible bully.

DRIPPER: Ooooooooohhhhh! I am scared. Getting your woman to fight for you now are you, Smith?

MIRANDA: Oh dear. Will you excuse me, Eddie? I think I'm going to have to sort this out.

[*She crosses to SC and stands facing* DRIPPER.]

MIRANDA: Now then. I'm going to count to ten and if you're not gone I shall have to take action, see?

DRIPPER: What?

MIRANDA: One, two, ten. Oh still here—bad luck.

[*She adopts karate pose.*]

MIRANDA: Hiiiiiiiii-yeeeeeeee-haaaaaaaahhhhh!!

[*Standing facing* DRIPPER *she starts whirling her right arm like a windmill. While he is watching this, she hits him in the stomach with her left hand, he doubles up, and she karate chops him on the back of the neck.*]

MIRANDA: Ah so!

[*Exit* MIRANDA *and* DRIPPER *SR.* EDDIE *crosses to home SL. Enter* MOTHER *SL.*]

EDDIE: I'm home.

MOTHER: Hello dear. Did you have a good day at school?

EDDIE: Not really, I got beaten up.

MOTHER: That's nice dear. [*Realising*] Did you say beaten up?

EDDIE: I'm afraid so.

MOTHER: Father! Father! Come quickly! Our Eddie's been in a fight!

[*Enter* FATHER *SL.*]

FATHER: Let me through I'm a doctor . . . accountant!

EDDIE: I'm all right, really I am.

FATHER: Son, you're not, you're black and blue . . . and pink and yellow and aubergine . . .

EDDIE: I'm sorry about last night.

FATHER: You were out late, son. Where did you go?

EDDIE: I went to church. Will you come with me sometime? I'd like that.

FATHER: Well I don't know, your Mother and I do like to get a good lie in . . . er . . . meditation on a Sunday morning.

EDDIE: I never asked you before, 'cos . . . well, it didn't mean so much to me before.

FATHER: Well, if it means that much to you . . .

EDDIE: Oh—it does. It's real now, I've stopped pretending. You can't go through life pretending, can you?

FATHER: No, you're right. You know I was saying that very same thing to the boys down the ranch. Yee harr! Dang my poons and horn my swaggles if we didn't round up a hundred head of cattle!

[*He spits. Unfortunately it hits* MOTHER.]

FATHER: Oh—sorry Mother!

[MOTHER *rushes off SL, followed by* FATHER.]

EDDIE: So that's it, really. Another day, another zit. But things have changed. Seems like, for me, just when I was at my lowest God picked me up and used me, only better than before. And all I had to do was ask. See you.

[*Exits SR.*]

Ophelia the Failure

Characters: OPHELIA—a girl who considers herself a failure.
PSYCHIATRIST—whom she consults.
DARREN—her boyfriend.
CUSTOMER—in shoe shop.
MANAGER—of shoe shop.
HEADMASTER—fearsome, shouts a lot.
BALLET TEACHER—Christian.

Plot: OPHELIA breaks up with her boyfriend, loses her Saturday job and fails to become a ballet dancer. She is finally reunited with her boyfriend after an abortive session with the school PSYCHIATRIST.

Main Point: That God loves us, despite our failures. That with him we are a success.

Running Time: 15 minutes.

Suitability: Evangelistic.

Staging: Chairs to represent the PSYCHIATRIST's couch SC, facing diagonally DSL. Chair behind couch for PSYCHIATRIST. Other action takes place SL and SR.

Props/Costumes: White coat, hammer for PSYCHIATRIST. Gown for HEADMASTER.

[*Enter* OPHELIA *and* PSYCHIATRIST. OPHELIA *lies down on the* PSYCHIATRIST'S *couch.*]

PSYCHIATRIST: Und zo—vat exactly iz ze problem?
OPHELIA: I'm a failure.
PSYCHIATRIST: So. You sink you're a failure?
OPHELIA: Yes.
PSYCHIATRIST: Vat exactly makes you sink zat?
OPHELIA: Life.
PSYCHIATRIST: Hmmm.

[*He tests her reflexes by hitting her knee. Nothing happens. He tries it again and her hand jerks up.*]

PSYCHIATRIST: Now, go to ze vindow and stick out your tongue.
OPHELIA: [*About to go and do it*] Will that help me?
PSYCHIATRIST: No, but it really annoys ze voman across ze road. I can't stand her.
OPHELIA: I never thought I'd have to consult the school psychiatrist.
PSYCHIATRIST: Oh, lots of people come to see me. People suffering from very deep fears—fears of alienation, fears zat everybody is out to get zem, fear of being bullied. Fear zat zeir friends vill make fun of zem.
OPHELIA: Wow. I never realised our pupils were so weird.
PSYCHIATRIST: No—zat's ze teachers. Ze pupils are even vorse. Anyway, how did all zese feelings of failure begin?
OPHELIA: I've known I'm a failure for years. Even my name tells me.
PSYCHIATRIST: Your name?
OPHELIA: Ophelia. Ophelia the failure.
PSYCHIATRIST: Zat is an unusual name.

OPHELIA: My parents were mad keen on Shakespeare at the time. They go through these phases. When my brother came along they were heavily into science fiction—that's why he's called Darth Vader O'Shaughnessy.

PSYCHIATRIST: I see.

OPHELIA: Anyway, I suppose things really came to a head last week. I . . . I broke off with my boyfriend.

[*Enter* DARREN *SR.* OPHELIA *gets up and stands, facing* DARREN.]

OPHELIA: There's another woman isn't there?

DARREN: What?

OPHELIA: There's another woman. You don't care about me any more.

DARREN: What are you on about now?

OPHELIA: Is she prettier than me?

DARREN: [*Joking*] Ophelia, I'm prettier than you.

OPHELIA: [*Crying*] That's a rotten thing to say!

DARREN: It was only a joke.

OPHELIA: It wasn't! It's true! I'm ugly! When I look in the mirror, it winces!

DARREN: You're not ugly!

OPHELIA: You said I was!

DARREN: Look, I wouldn't go out with an ugly woman would I?

OPHELIA So you don't want to go out with me then?

DARREN: [*Confused*] I didn't say that.

OPHELIA: Yes you did. You said I'm ugly, and then you said you wouldn't go out with an ugly woman which means you don't want to go out with me!

DARREN: I wish I knew how your mind works. It was a joke.

OPHELIA: So that's how you see our relationship is it? A joke? Well in that case Darren Puke you can leave. Get away! Never darken my doorstep again!

DARREN: Right—well if that's how you want it. I'm going!

[Goes to leave SR. Then stops.]

DARREN: Wait a minute—this is my house.

OPHELIA: Well in that case—never darken your own doorstep again. So there.

[Exit DARREN. OPHELIA *lies down on the couch again.]*

OPHELIA: So you see, we split up.

PSYCHIATRIST: I see. Vell, ze explanation is very simple. You split up vis Darren because you have a deep-seated introverted personality rejection disorder.

OPHELIA: Oh. How simple. What does that mean?

PSYCHIATRIST: You sink you're a failure.

OPHELIA: Brilliant.

PSYCHIATRIST: Und zis feeling makes you destroy sings before zey have a chance to go wrong. You sink zat zey vill always go wrong because nothing you do ever goes right.

OPHELIA: That's it! Nothing ever goes right. I mean—that was on Friday night and on Saturday I went to start a new job in a shoe shop. A Saturday job.

[Enter CUSTOMER. OPHELIA *kneels at her feet and brings shoes from under couch.* CUSTOMER *has been trying on shoes.]*

CUSTOMER: No, I don't think these will do.

OPHELIA: Oh, haven't you got funny shaped feet? All bumpy.

CUSTOMER: I'm sorry?

OPHELIA: Your feet. I was just commenting. This is my first day here.

CUSTOMER: You do surprise me.

OPHELIA: Mind you—I shouldn't think I'll stay here long [*Picks up* CUSTOMER'*s shoes*] not if these are the kind of thing we're selling! I mean look at them—great clumpy things—you'd have to be a complete moron to wear these wouldn't you? A tasteless moron at that! Now, where did I put your shoes?

CUSTOMER: You're holding them.

OPHELIA: [*Pause*] Ah.

CUSTOMER: A tasteless moron, eh?

OPHELIA: [*Rising*] Let's not get upset . . .

CUSTOMER: [*Putting shoes back on*] I wish to see the manager.

OPHELIA: You can't! That is . . . he . . . he's not here.

CUSTOMER: Not here?

OPHELIA: He's ill. Rushed to hospital. A pair of walking boots fell on his head.

CUSTOMER: I demand to see the manager.

[*Enter* MANAGER.]

MANAGER: Anything wrong Madam?

CUSTOMER: This . . . this *thing* has just insulted me!

MANAGER: Insulted you? Ophelia, what's all this about?

OPHELIA: It was just a mistake . . .

CUSTOMER: She called me a tasteless moron!

MANAGER: Is this true?

OPHELIA: Well only by accident . . .

MANAGER: You will apologise at once.

OPHELIA: I will not.

MANAGER: [*Taking her aside*] Apologise before I take a pair of size ten Doc Martens and shove one up each of your nostrils.

OPHELIA: [*Reluctantly, to* CUSTOMER] I'm sorry I called you a tasteless moron, but let's face it, the truth had to come out sooner or later.

MANAGER: Ophelia!

CUSTOMER: I've never been so insulted in my life!

OPHELIA: You ought to get out more.

CUSTOMER: How dare you!

OPHELIA: [*To* MANAGER] Well good heavens, look at her, she's got feet like Donald Duck! I can't do miracles you know, I mean I'm only supposed to sell shoes. You can get flippers from the sports shop.

MANAGER: Ophelia, you are fired.

OPHELIA: What? Fired? But it's the truth!

MANAGER: You're still fired.

OPHELIA: I'm being repressed for speaking the truth.

MANAGER: [*Losing temper*] Look, you know she's a tasteless moron, and I know she's a tasteless moron, but we're not supposed to let her know that!

CUSTOMER: I am not a tasteless moron.

MANAGER: You keep out of this you great tasteless lump!

CUSTOMER: That does it!

[*Smashes* MANAGER *over the head with her umbrella. Exit* MANAGER *SR and* CUSTOMER, *SL.* OPHELIA *faces* PSYCHIATRIST.]

PSYCHIATRIST: Zo vot happened after zat?

OPHELIA: Well, the manager had to go to hospital, and when he regained consciousness all he could mutter was 'sack Ophelia'. I left. Quickly.

PSYCHIATRIST: Quite right.

OPHELIA: [*Sitting on the couch and facing the audience*] Oh I don't know. I'm too young to be in psycho-analysis.

PSYCHIATRIST: Nonsense. You are never too young. Tell me, vot kind of dreams do you have?

OPHELIA: I had a weird dream last night. I dreamt I was running through this swamp, being chased by crocodiles and they were getting nearer and nearer, and then I tripped and fell into the water, only it wasn't water it was raspberry jam, and this crocodile came up and grabbed me and then it changed into Rick Astley [*or whoever is trendy*] and then . . . then . . . no it's too horrible.

PSYCHIATRIST: Vot?

OPHELIA: He *sang* to me.

PSYCHIATRIST: Vot a hideous nightmare.

OPHELIA: Yes. It was worse than being eaten. What does it all mean?

PSYCHIATRIST: Crocodiles . . . swamps . . . raspberry jam . . . it means you have a deep seated fear of becoming an estate agent.

OPHELIA: Are you sure?

PSYCHIATRIST: Not positive, no. Und zen vot happened?

OPHELIA: Well, Sunday I was just depressed. And Monday morning the head gave us all one of his 'assembly' talks. All about the impending exams.

[OPHELIA *lies still on couch. Enter* HEADMASTER, SR. *Moves about DSC.*]

HEADMASTER: Good morning, school. Today I want to bring to your attention some interesting facts about exams. One, if you don't revise you don't pass. Two, if you don't pass you will be cast into the outer darkness of unemployment for ever to be a lost statistic in an uncaring world. Your life will fall apart, no-one will talk to you again, and you will probably die a painful death. Failure is not a nice thing to contemplate, not unlike you Blenkinsop—if you must blow your nose use a hankie and not the hair of the girl in front. Where was I? Ah yes, failure is a spectre that haunts us all—Blenkinsop, stop scratching yourself. Yes, we must strive for . . . I didn't mean you could start scratching other people, boy. See me afterwards. Remember, if you are a failure no one will want to talk to you ever again. Assembly dismissed.

[*Exit* HEADMASTER, *SR.*]

OPHELIA: [*Sitting up*] Of course, he may have been laying it on a bit thick.

PSYCHIATRIST: But his talk made you worried?

OPHELIA: Yes.

PSYCHIATRIST: Even zo you are possibly ze cleverest pupil in ze school? Even zo you are ze only pupil in ze school doing GCSE Atomic Research?

OPHELIA: I'm a born failure. Why should the exams be any different? It's just like ballet.

[*She gets up and moves one chair over to SR to use as 'barre'.*]

PSYCHIATRIST: Ballet?

OPHELIA: My ballet class last night. That was the final straw. See—ever since I was young, I've wanted to go to ballet school.

[*Enter* TEACHER, *SR. Crosses to SC. During this conversation,* OPHELIA *practises pliés, exercises etc.*]

TEACHER: Ophelia, I'm going to level with you. You are never going to make it into ballet school.

OPHELIA: But I'm trying!

TEACHER: For one thing, pupils enter at twelve. You are now four years late.

OPHELIA: I wouldn't mind going back to the start.

TEACHER: You simply haven't got the right build.

OPHELIA: I could diet.

TEACHER: Ophelia, to get down to the required weight for a prima ballerina you would have to do more than diet—you would have to cut one of your legs off.

OPHELIA: I could try.

TEACHER: [*Finally coming clean*] Ophelia, you're not good enough!

OPHELIA: [*Shocked*] Not good . . .

TEACHER: Look, only a tiny percentage of girls get to the Royal Ballet School—and of them only one or two will ever be more than talented amateurs. There simply aren't the jobs around.

OPHELIA: Then I've failed . . .

TEACHER: No you haven't. You've simply recognised your limitations.

OPHELIA: [*Bitterly*] Ophelia the failure strikes again.

TEACHER: Don't feel like that. I mean, who of us hasn't failed at some time?

OPHELIA: But you don't understand . . .

TEACHER: I understand that you feel everything you touch turns to clay. But you're not special that way . . . look—do you believe in God?

OPHELIA: What's that got to do with it?

TEACHER: It might help.

OPHELIA: When I was a kid I suppose . . . I don't know really.

TEACHER: It's just that, well, I'm a Christian you see, and for me it always helps to know that whatever I do, whatever happens, God will always love me. He . . . he cares about my life. He helps me to disregard the failures, because I know as long as he loves me I'll be a success.

OPHELIA: But I want to be a dancer!

[*She twirls and gives a quick 'balletic' run across to DSL.*]

TEACHER: Well give up on that. You have all the grace of a bull hippo.

OPHELIA: You're not very helpful for a Christian. You're supposed to give me comfort and sympathy.

TEACHER: You don't need it. You just need to grow up.

[*Exit* TEACHER, *SR.* PSYCHIATRIST *is snoring, gently.*]

OPHELIA: [*Sitting at left end of couch*] And that was that. So what do you think I should do about it?

PSYCHIATRIST: [*Waking up*] Vot? Vot happened? Ah . . . ah yes . . . now . . . zis is a complex problem. Vot we have to do is . . . is . . . vell I can't actually sink of anysink at ze moment . . . you'll just have to live vis it.

OPHELIA: What—you mean I'll always be a failure?

PSYCHIATRIST: Vell, I feel a failure most of my life, vy should you be any different?

OPHELIA: But you're supposed to help me!

PSYCHIATRIST: So? I failed. Zat's ze vay ze sauerkraut crumbles you know.

OPHELIA: You're nothing but a phoney!

PSYCHIATRIST: Zere is no need to get excited.

OPHELIA: And stop talking in that ridiculous German accent! Everybody knows you come from Orpington.

PSYCHIATRIST: [*Dropping accent*] Well—ah—it's just a gimmick. Helps trade ... [*Putting it back on again*] Und it helps me concentrate.

OPHELIA: You're useless! No-one can help me.

PSYCHIATRIST: Vell, vot about your dance teacher? She sounded sensible ...

OPHELIA: What—all that God stuff?

PSYCHIATRIST: Isn't it important to know zat someone vill love you, even ven you don't succeed? Isn't zat vot ve all vant?

OPHELIA: I'm not listening to you any more, you fake. I'm going.

[*Exit* PSYCHIATRIST. OPHELIA *begins to exit SR and meets* DARREN *coming on.*]

DARREN: Oh—it's you.

OPHELIA: Yeah—it's me.

DARREN: You all right?

OPHELIA: [*Faking*] Oh yeah, fine, fine. Never better.

DARREN: Oh. I heard about the ballet ...

OPHELIA: Did you?

DARREN: Shame. I know you had your heart set on that.

OPHELIA: Yeah. Well. It's just one of those things.

DARREN: Listen, I was wondering ... you wouldn't like to go to see a film tonight would you? I mean I haven't got anything better to do, and I got given this spare ticket.

OPHELIA: Darren Puke, you are the most thick-headed, lame-brained, pathetic chatter-upper I have ever met.

DARREN: Is that yes or no?

OPHELIA: Yes. Please.

DARREN: Brilliant.

OPHELIA: [*Sitting on left end of couch*] Do you know what the school psychiatrist said? He said

I chucked you because I was scared it wasn't going to work out.

DARREN: That's daft.

OPHELIA: It's more than daft. It's accurate.

DARREN: [*Joining her on couch*] But what about all the good times we had eh? What about Vanessa's party?

OPHELIA: Yeah. That was fun.

DARREN: Or when we went skating and you fell through the ice?

OPHELIA: That wasn't a good time!

DARREN: It was! It was fun! You take all your failures too seriously. I mean fancy only lasting thirteen minutes in the shoe shop before you got sacked!

OPHELIA: Yeah, I suppose it is funny . . .

DARREN: We've had some great times, and just cause you're going through a rough patch, doesn't mean we've got to stop going out does it?

OPHELIA: No, you're right. We have had some good times. And we can have plenty more.

DARREN: Of course, the best time of all was in the cinema. During the power cut.

OPHELIA: Oh yes . . . [*realising*] wait a minute, I don't remember that!

DARREN: Oh. Must've been someone else.

OPHELIA: [*Standing up and whacking* DARREN *on the shoulder*] Darren! How could you? I'm never going to speak to you again!
[OPHELIA *exits SR.*]

DARREN: It was just a joke!

OPHELIA: [*Shouted from offstage*] You philanderer!

DARREN: [*Shouting after her*] I was just joking . . . oh what's the use? Here we go again.
[*He exits, SR.*]

All the Fun of the Fair

Characters:	ANGEL—bizarre, eccentric but likeable. JANICE—heroine. Insecure. MOTHER—stern. BRENDA—radical feminist. Aggressive. TONY MORRIS—a bit of a lad. Egotistical.
Plot:	JANICE goes to the fun fair, where she meets an angel and learns to like herself.
Main Point:	That God loves us, as we are. That sometimes we hate ourselves.
Running Time:	20 minutes.
Suitability:	Evangelistic, teenage event.
Staging:	Chair for the ANGEL to sit on when he's not taking part in the action. Chairs to form the Tunnel of Love, Roundabout etc.
Props/Costumes:	Waistcoat, flat cap, money bag for ANGEL. Combat jacket and loads of badges for BRENDA. Sunglasses and book for TONY. Coconuts and bean bags for coconut shy; big balloon for test-your-strength machine.
Remarks:	Sound effects play an important part in this. They need to be very loud and very precise. The sketch can

also be introduced and ended with music. We used Bruce Springsteen's 'Tunnel of Love'.

ANGEL: Roll up! Roll up! For all the fun of the fair! Sit back, and for the next twenty minutes let me take you on a roller coaster ride through an evening in the life of Janice! Experience all the thrills and spills of the fair as we ride on the big dipper, have a shy at the coconuts, ride on the dodgems and, of course, enter the tunnel of love. But we start our journey in the wild, wacky hall of mirrors!

[ANGEL *sits USL. Enter* JANICE. *She is plucking her eyebrows.*]

JANICE: Ouch. Why am I doing this? I am using a pair of metal tweezers to pull hairs from my face, causing myself excruciating pain, in the belief that it makes me look beautiful. In the cause of beauty I shave my legs, plaster myself with cosmetics, dye my hair, pluck my eyebrows and paint my toenails. If I did that to an animal I'd get reported to the RSPCA.

MUM: [*Offstage*] Haven't you finished in there yet? Your father wants to use the bathroom.

JANICE: When I look in the mirror I see a stranger. Ohhh. My hair's so greasy. I wish I could look like them girls in the adverts—all sultry and oozing sex. [*She tries a few sultry looks*] Looks like I'm having a bad attack of indigestion.

MUM: For heaven's sake hurry up! Your father needs to use the bathroom!

JANICE: I don't have many friends. Not real friends. People feel sorry for me. No—come on, be positive. You are OK. You are nice. [*Depressed*] Ohhhhh.

MUM: Janice! If your father doesn't use the bathroom this minute, something terrible's going to happen.

JANICE: [*To* MUM] Yeah, yeah, in a minute. [*To herself*] Maybe you'll get a date. Maybe Tony Morris will ask you out. Maybe a squadron of pigs will fly past.

MUM: Janice! For heaven's sake!

JANICE: Why is it other girls get so many dates? Oh well, here we go. Right, bathroom's free.

[*Sound effect: There is a huge explosion.*]

JANICE: [*Opening the door*] What's happened?

MUM: [*Entering*] Too late. Next time you spend three hours in the bathroom, kindly do it on a night when your father hasn't just had a vindaloo special extra hot takeaway.

JANICE: Where is he?

MUM: He's about four houses down the road. The force of the blast blew him out through the landing window.

[*Exit* JANICE *and* MUM.]

ANGEL: [*Rising and moving DSL.*] Poor old Janice. Sixteen years old and already depressed. Life for her is a constant struggle to feel good about herself. A roller-coaster ride where there are more downs than ups.

[*Enter* BRENDA. *She stands SC, waiting for* JANICE *who arrives from USR, out of breath.*]

JANICE: Oh—hello Brenda. Sorry I'm late. Dad had a Vindaloo extra hot and he exploded. There was a heck of a mess and we had to call the fire brigade to get him down off a lamp-post where he'd ended up.

BRENDA: Is he all right?

JANICE: Oh yes. He's really accident prone. He's broken his leg, fractured his skull and lost all his hair. And that was just last week.

ANGEL: I know what you're wondering—why can't they see me?

[*He moves round the back of* BRENDA *and* JANICE *and stands between them.*]

ANGEL: Well, never mind me, what about you lot? I mean a whole load of people sitting there watching them, you'd think they'd notice. Anyway, if I wanted to be seen, I've only got to click my fingers.

[*Clicks his fingers.*]

ANGEL: Ooops, not yet.

[*Clicks his fingers again.*]

JANICE: That's funny. I thought I saw a man appear out of nowhere. Must have been wishful thinking.

BRENDA: Wishful thinking? Nightmare more like. Men are such pigs.

JANICE: Well—not all men.

BRENDA: Oh, you're so oppressed you don't even realise it. Women only need men for one thing—to keep the human race going.

JANICE: Well, surely there's more to it than that.

BRENDA: If this world was run by women do you think we'd have all the wars that go on? Do you think we'd have all the selfishness and greed? If this country were run by a woman do you think we'd have the atomic bomb?

JANICE: Brenda, this country is run by a woman.

BRENDA: Yeah, well, sort of.

JANICE: Anyway, of course we'd have all the trouble. Women can be just as selfish as men.

BRENDA: Oh, you've been brainwashed!

[*Enter* TONY, *SR. He wolf-whistles at the girls.*]

JANICE: There's Tony Morris. Isn't he gorgeous?

BRENDA: Huh!

TONY: Hello darling!

BRENDA: Bigot.

[ANGEL *clicks his fingers and appears, DSL. He is holding a balloon.*]

ANGEL: Roll up! Come on gents! Try your hand at the test-your-strength machine. Mr Morris, can I tempt you to try your hand?

TONY: How come you know my name?

ANGEL: Oh everyone knows you, Mr Morris. You are famed throughout the town for your good looks, charm and savoir faire.

TONY: You what?

ANGEL: Well, maybe just your good looks then.

[ANGEL *holds up balloon and becomes test-your-strength machine. He gives results in a robot-like voice.*]

TONY: Yeah, all right I'll have a go.

[TONY *crosses to SL and tries his hand.*]

ANGEL: You have scored five out of ten. Wimpo.

TONY: Yeah, well, I wasn't really trying was I? Just one hand that was. Feast your eyes on this!

[*He hits it again.*]

ANGEL: You have scored six out of ten. Weed.

TONY: Stupid machine. Must be something wrong with it.

JANICE: Six out of ten's not bad.

TONY: Yeah well, I weren't really putting everything into it, was I? I mean this is what I can do when I really try.

[*He gives the balloon a massive strike, pauses for a moment and disintegrates into agony over his damaged fingers.*]

ANGEL: You have scored ten out of ten and crippled yourself. You are strong, but stupid.

[TONY *continues to whimper in agony.*]

JANICE: Are you all right?

TONY: 'Course I am. Just an old wound that's all. Knife fight.

BRENDA: Show off.

TONY: [*To* JANICE] What are you doing tonight then?

JANICE: Oh—nothing.

TONY: Well in that case go and buy some chips, I want to talk to your friend.

JANICE: Oh.

TONY: [*To* BRENDA] Hello darling.

BRENDA: You talking to me?

TONY: Fancy a date then?

BRENDA: I don't go out with loud-mouthed chauvinistic pigs.

[TONY *kisses her passionately.*]

BRENDA: Ohhhh, well all right, just this once.

[*They exit, SR, arms around each other.*]

JANICE: [*Angry*] Ohhhhhhh!!!

[*She hits the balloon in temper.* ANGEL *releases the balloon and it zooms off into the audience.*]

ANGEL: [*As machine*] You have scored eleven out of ten. You are probably the Incredible Hulk.

[*Exit* JANICE, *SR.*]

ANGEL: Jilted! Oh the pains of young love! What better therefore to relieve the pain we feel by throwing things at others. All change.

[*Clicks his fingers.*]

ANGEL: You want a go on the coconut shy, Miss?

JANICE: Good idea. All right, coconuts—prepare to die.

[*The* ANGEL *stands, arms outstretched, holding a coconut in each hand. He is now the coconut shy. Clever, isn't it?*]

ANGEL: You on your own then?

JANICE: [*Depressed*] Yeah. [*Bluffing*] I mean I could have gone out with any number of blokes tonight. Just didn't feel like it, that's all.

ANGEL: Of course.

JANICE: I'm not like some people. Some people claim to have high principles.

[*Throws bag at* ANGEL.]

JANICE: Then they run off with any Tom, Dick or Tony. Tongue hanging out, drooling, it's disgusting . . .

[*Throws again. It hits him again.*]

ANGEL: Right.

JANICE: Of course I never really liked her. I saw through her at once. Man-eater.

[*Throws again.*]

ANGEL: [*Crossing to* JANICE] You're not a very good shot are you? You're all anger and no accuracy.

[*He gives the coconuts to* JANICE.]

JANICE: Oh no, they're coming. I'm off.

[JANICE *exits SR.* TONY *and* BRENDA *enter SL.*]

ANGEL: And so she disappears showing us a good example of the dodgems. Relationships are like the Helter Skelter. We start so high and descend so quickly.

[TONY *and* BRENDA *stand in the middle of stage, hugging.*]

ANGEL: Ah, romance! What could be better? A warm summer evening, the scent of honeysuckle on the night air. Millions of stars twinkling in the velvety blue darkness. Two bodies in warm embrace.

TONY: Come on then, give us a snog.

BRENDA: Oh leave it out, Tony!

[ANGEL *clicks his fingers again. Moves chairs to CS.*]

ANGEL: Roll up ladies, and, for want of a better word,

gentleman. The tunnel of love awaits you. Two tickets, sir?

TONY: Good in there is it?

ANGEL: Wonderful sir, very romantic.

TONY: Yeah, well, as long as it's dark I don't mind. Know what I mean?

ANGEL: You really are neanderthal, aren't you sir?

TONY: No—I'm Gemini.

BRENDA: What we doing?

TONY: Tunnel of love, innit?

[*He guides her to a chair.*]

ANGEL: [*Taking* TONY *aside*] Er, before you go in, sir. Tell me, how come such an obnoxious nurk like yourself has such powers over the fairer sex?

TONY: What?

ANGEL: How do you get the birds?

TONY: Oh, simple. I use the book.

ANGEL: Book?

TONY: My manual.

[TONY *takes a book from his pocket and hands it to the* ANGEL.]

ANGEL: [*Reading*] 'The Observers Book of Birds. Tips and Hints on Pulling the Bints'. Remarkable. I didn't even know you could read.

TONY: Tells you all you need to know. Now clear off, eh? I got to get cracking.

[TONY *sits on the chair next to* BRENDA. *They pause for a moment, looking straight ahead, and then* TONY *leaps on* BRENDA.]

BRENDA: [*Fighting him off*] Leave it out!

TONY: Oh go on!

BRENDA: I am not a toy. I am not an object. I am a free independent woman.

TONY: Give us a kiss.

[*They kiss.*]

BRENDA: But even radical feminists need affection sometimes.

TONY: Yeah. [*Mutters to himself*] Where's me manual? [*He has his arms round* BRENDA *and reads the manual over her shoulder*.]

TONY: Let me tell you something my angel . . .

BRENDA: What?

TONY: I really love you insert name of bird.

BRENDA: Eh?

TONY: Oh, I see. I really love you . . . [*he looks at label of* BRENDA*'s jacket*] Dorothy Perkins.

BRENDA: Brenda!

TONY: That as well. Anyway—I really love you.

BRENDA: Do you really?

TONY: Yeah. I think you're really special, Blender.

BRENDA: Brenda.

TONY: And I want to have your children . . . wait a minute that can't be right.

BRENDA: Isn't this romantic? Not, of course, that I care for romance, as it is merely a tool for the enslavement of women. But if I did, and it wasn't, then this is.

TONY: Er . . . right. [*Reading*] Oh Blender . . . Brenda. I've never felt this way before with any other woman. I wish we could stay this way for ever.

BRENDA: Oh Tony, is it true, what you're saying? Do you really feel this way?

TONY: Oh, how I've adored you from a farm. Afar.

BRENDA: I never knew! Oh Tony!

[ANGEL *moves in front of them, blocking them from the audience. Exit* TONY *and* BRENDA.]

ANGEL: And so we draw a discreet veil over this unsavoury scene. Meanwhile—back on the merry-go-round, Janice is discovering that, just when she thought she was getting somewhere, she's right back where she started.

[*Enter* JANICE *SR. She turns a chair round and sits on it, as if on a carousel horse.*]

ANGEL: [*Doing same*] Fares please.

JANICE: Oh right . . . are you following me?

ANGEL: What makes you think that?

JANICE: Well, first you were on the test-your-strength machine, then you were on the coconut shy and now you're here. Either this fairground is very short-staffed or something strange is going on.

ANGEL: Actually, something strange is going on.

JANICE: Who are you?

ANGEL: I work for the person who made all this.

JANICE: What—the merry-go-round?

ANGEL: No [*gesturing*] all this.

JANICE: But that's the common.

ANGEL: Exactly.

JANICE: But no-one made the common. It just happened.

ANGEL: No, God made the common.

JANICE: You're a nutter aren't you?

ANGEL: Yes. He's very fond of nutters is God. He collects them. He's got a planet full of them.

JANICE: Just my luck. The only guy interested in me is a complete fruitcake. I'm off.

[*She gets off the carousel and walks clockwise around the stage. The* ANGEL *moves DS.*]

ANGEL: Some people take a lot of persuading, you know.

[*He clicks his fingers and 'appears' right in front of* JANICE, *who is approaching CS from SL.*]

ANGEL: Hello.

JANICE: How did you do that? You just . . . appeared.

ANGEL: Did I? It's all done with mirrors. Now we must talk.

JANICE: Look, who are you?

ANGEL: You wouldn't believe me if I told you.

JANICE: Yes, I would.

ANGEL: No, you wouldn't.

JANICE: Yes, I would.

ANGEL: I'm an angel.

JANICE: I don't believe you.

ANGEL: Your name is Janice Roberts. You live at 28, Acacia Avenue.

JANICE: Well, anyone could tell you that.

ANGEL: Your middle name is Mildred.

JANICE: Shhhh! I've been trying to keep that a secret for years. Anyway, you could have looked that up in the records or something.

ANGEL: You have a mole on your left . . .

JANICE: [*Interrupting*] All right, all right I believe you. Really? An angel?

ANGEL: If only the people knew how many of us there were around they'd be scared to walk down the street. [*An invisible colleague bumps into him*] Oi! Watch where you're going! [*To Janice*] You're not convinced, are you?

JANICE: No.

ANGEL: Well—what would it take to convince you?

JANICE: I dunno. Something pretty big like a heavenly chorus or something.

[*The angel clicks his fingers and one 'Hallelujah' from the Hallelujah chorus blares out.*]

ANGEL: I'm more into hip-hop myself, but give the public what they want, that's what I say.

JANICE: But why would an angel be interested in me?

ANGEL: Look around you, what do you see?

JANICE: A dump.

ANGEL: Nothing is a dump. Everything is beautiful. Potentially. Look at that.

JANICE: That's a slag heap.

ANGEL: And what is on that slag heap?

JANICE: An old bicycle tyre. A tin can. Oh and a daisy.

ANGEL: Exactly. A daisy! Just imagine what that slag heap would look like if it was covered with daisies!

JANICE: [*After thinking for a moment*] It would look like a slag heap with daisies on it.

ANGEL: You certainly used your imagination there, didn't you? It would be beautiful. You really hate yourself, don't you?

JANICE: What's there to like?

ANGEL: You look at yourself and only see a slag heap.

JANICE: Charming.

ANGEL: You don't see the good bits. You only see the rubbish—the tin cans, the bicycle tyres . . .

JANICE: That's all there is, I'm all rubbish.

ANGEL: Oh shut up! Let me tell you, when God looks at you, he thinks you're beautiful.

JANICE: Go on.

ANGEL: No, he does—he's daft like that. Oh, he sees the bad bits as well, but he still thinks you're beautiful. And anyway, if you ask him, he'll get rid of the bad bits just like that.

[*Clicks his fingers and disappears.* JANICE *looks bewildered.*]

ANGEL: Oh, sorry.

[*Clicks his fingers and 'returns'.*]

JANICE: How do you do that?

ANGEL: It's all in the wrist action.

JANICE: Why are you telling me all this?

ANGEL: Because God wants you to know. I mean, he could have told you himself, but I get such a kick out of humans he allowed me to have a go. God's dead keen on you, you know. He really loves you. And he wants you to tell your friends.

[JANICE *turns away during next speech.* ANGEL

clicks his fingers and 'disappears'. He sits SL. BRENDA *enters SR.*]

JANICE: But how do I know you're real? How do I know you're not a figment of my imagination? How do I know you're not an hallucination caused by eating too much candy floss?

BRENDA: What are you on about?

JANICE: Oh—where'd he go? He was right here!

BRENDA: Who? Oh, what does it matter who. Men! They're all the same!

JANICE: What happened?

BRENDA: Tony chucked me.

JANICE: That didn't last long. You've only been going out twenty-five minutes.

BRENDA: I've been used. I was a fool. A weak fool.

JANICE: Don't be upset.

BRENDA: I'm not upset. I am a strong woman. I'm not upset.

JANICE: Good.

BRENDA: [*Hideously upset*] I just want to diiiiieeeeee!!!!!

JANICE: There, there. Look, you don't have to worry. God loves you. God loves all of us.

BRENDA: Oh yeah? Not me.

JANICE: No, he does. He loves us all.

BRENDA: How do you know?

JANICE: This angel told me.

BRENDA: Brilliant.

JANICE: [*Searching for inspiration*] Look, you are like . . . like that slag heap over there.

BRENDA: Oh noooooooooo!!!!

JANICE: Ah. Probably not the best thing to say under the circumstances. Come on, let's go and get some tea.

[*She starts to take* BRENDA *off SR, but turns the other way because* TONY *is coming.* BRENDA *exits SL.*]

JANICE: Oops—other way. You go on ahead.

TONY: Oh. She's a bit upset.

JANICE: You could say that.

TONY: Well, it was never going to work. We were incompetent.

JANICE: Incompatible.

TONY: That an' all. Listen, what are you doing for the rest of the evening?

JANICE: Sorry?

TONY: Well, you know, I'm free—you're free. How about getting together and making six?

[*He laughs at his own joke.* JANICE *smiles, the kind of smile to be seen on the face of a cat before it leaps on some poor, unsuspecting bird. She goes very close to* TONY, *grabs the belt of his trousers and pulls upwards, causing him to rise on tip-toes.*]

JANICE: Now listen and listen good. I've just found out that God loves me and therefore I should love you because I should love my neighbour, even though he is an insignificant little toe-rag with the IQ of a retarded newt! But if you ever try and mess with me or my friend again I will tear you into little pieces, understand?

[TONY *squeaks and nods.*]

JANICE: Good.

[*She releases the belt and* TONY *collapses onto the floor.*]

JANICE: And that's only because I care about you. I'm going home.

[*She exits SR.*]

TONY: I think I'm in love. Where's me manual?

[*Hurriedly starts looking through book.* ANGEL *clicks fingers and stands behind* TONY.]

ANGEL: Why don't you forget about the book, eh?

TONY: Oh, it's you. Where did you spring from?

ANGEL: Assignment three billion and four, Morris, Tony. [*Looks upwards*] Look, I know I like dealing with humans, but are you sure he counts? I mean you've got to have some basic stuff to start with . . .

TONY: What are you on about?

ANGEL: Tony—it's time for you to change. Have you ever heard of God?

TONY: Of course I have. I had some for tea with chips.

ANGEL: This is going to be more difficult than I thought.

[*They exit.*]

LESSON FOUR

DUOS

Like group work, a lot depends on you having the right number of people to act in these pieces, namely, two. We did try them with three, but one person just ended up hanging around and looking stupid.

These pieces explore a number of themes, all of which seem hardly worth going into here. The important thing to remember about two-handers, as they are called in the trade, is that they must always be played as small, intimate moments; little vignettes; tiny cameos; life in miniature; wee, titchy, pocket-sized, Lilliputian, dinky, little scenes. Unless, of course, they are *big*. In which case ignore all I've just said.

One other little trick of the trade which might help you. If the other person in the sketch stops talking, then it's *your* turn.

The Wedding

Characters:	BRIDE GROOM
Plot:	The miracle at Cana, from the point of view of the bride and groom.
Main Point:	That Jesus can take ordinary things and transform them.
Running time:	5 minutes.
Suitability:	Church event.
Props/Costumes:	Veil for BRIDE. GROOM wears a bow tie and a frock coat if possible. Knife. Box with horrible gift in it.

[*At beginning* BRIDE *and* GROOM *pose, holding the knife as if they were being photographed cutting the wedding cake.*]

GROOM: Well, it's all going very well so far.
BRIDE: And what do you mean by that?
GROOM: I should have thought it was obvious. Dear.
BRIDE: So all this is my fault?
GROOM: Well, I didn't make the catering arrangements.
BRIDE: It's not my fault.
GROOM: Why do I get this strange sense of foreboding? Why do I get the feeling that those words are going to recur throughout my marriage?

BRIDE: I think you're being perfectly horrible.

[*They pause and smile for another photo, then resume.*]

GROOM: Look, they're beginning to notice.

BRIDE: Perhaps they won't mind.

[GROOM *puts knife away SL.* BRIDE *preens herself SL and arranges herself as if for a photo.*]

GROOM: Oh no, of course they won't. Pardon me, I hope you're all enjoying the reception. I know it's ninety degrees outside but you won't notice if we don't give you any more wine, will you? Just sit there and bake like good little guests.

BRIDE: Maybe we could make up some story—like it's part of the new Roman anti-drink and drive campaign. You know—leave the chariot at home and all that.

GROOM: I'm not a complete idiot you know.

BRIDE: Oh, is there a bit missing then?

GROOM: Oh, very witty.

BRIDE: Well, you come up with a better idea.

[*She walks across to* GROOM *SC and flicks dust from his jacket, etc. They end up side by side looking diagonally DSR for another photo.*]

GROOM: Let's just analyse the situation logically, shall we? We have just run out of wine. We have a hundred and fifty guests, waiting for refills.

BRIDE: What do we do then?

GROOM: Panic.

[*Both grin for another photo.*]

BRIDE: So much for logic.

GROOM: But where could it have gone to? I know. Your mother drank it.

BRIDE: Don't be ridiculous.

GROOM: No, it's the only explanation—a hundred and fifty guests expecting maybe three more glasses each, that's four hundred and fifty glasses—piece of cake to your mother. She could knock back four hundred and fifty glasses in a lunchtime.

BRIDE: That's right. Pick on my family.

GROOM: Well, good grief, look at them! They've descended on this feast like a plague of locusts. I'm surprised they haven't eaten the furniture. I know—they're another plague. Yes, that's it! Eleven plagues there were—blood, hail, boils, locusts, frogs, gnats, flies, sickness, darkness, killing of the first born. And the Rosenthal family.

[He goes to fetch present from USC.]

BRIDE: I never knew you could be so horrible.

[Opens and looks at the wedding present.]

GROOM: Talking of horrible.

BRIDE: *[Putting present away]* Yes, well, I always said your aunt's taste was atrocious.

[The aunt just happens to walk by at that moment. They smile sweetly at her.]

BRIDE: Hello, Auntie, we were just talking about you . . . enjoying it? Good. Wine? Yes, yes they're just opening up a few more barrels of the stuff. Be along in a minute. . . . Yes, have a nice time. . . . Look at her. The human sponge. You talk about my family.

GROOM: That is my auntie you're insulting.

BRIDE: What about that other lot who came? The teacher.

GROOM: They're old friends of the family.

BRIDE: Oh, yeah. Weirdos.

GROOM: He's not weird.

BRIDE: Oh no. He gives up a perfectly good carpenter's job to wander around the countryside preaching. No wonder he turned up for the free food.

GROOM: He came because I invited him. Foolishly, I thought it would be a happy cheerful occasion. An occasion full of fun and festivity, and not a full meeting of the Cana teetotallers society.

BRIDE: It's not my fault. It's the caterers. And he's brought a load of fishermen with him!

GROOM: What's wrong with that? They're good blokes.

BRIDE: Have you smelt them? One of them came up to congratulate me. It was like kissing a pilchard.

GROOM: What's he doing now? [*Looking over at waiter*] Oh, no . . .

BRIDE: What are they doing? That's the washing-up water! They're serving up the washing-up water!

GROOM: Don't panic. There has to be some very good reason why all our guests and relatives are about to get dysentery.

BRIDE: But that's the water for . . . It's not for drinking! Oh no. [*To waiter*] Er, excuse me . . . why are you serving us the dishwater? Ha! [*To husband*] He says it's been miraculously turned to wine. Now listen, if you don't come up with the goods soon, I will miraculously turn you and your catering firm into a random collection of separate limbs.

GROOM: That goes for me too!

[*He picks up glass from floor DSC and tastes some wine.*]

BRIDE: Run a wedding reception? They couldn't run a bath. What's up with you?

[*Groom points, speechless, towards the wine.*]

BRIDE: You haven't drunk some have you?

GROOM: It's wonderful!

BRIDE: Are you having some kind of breakdown?

GROOM: It's wine!

BRIDE: Good grief!

GROOM: He did it! Jesus! He turned the washing-up water into wine.

BRIDE: [*Tasting the wine*] Hmmm. Not bad. A good nose to it and I'm fairly amused by its precociousness.

GROOM: But . . . this is a miracle! At our wedding!

BRIDE: Yes, well there's no need to go over the top, darling . . . I wonder how he does it?

GROOM: What does that matter? What does it matter how? I mean he took something ordinary and turned it into something special! He couldn't do something with your mother, could he?

BRIDE: Now, don't start! We must go and thank him.

GROOM: Yes . . . here, Jesus! You couldn't rustle up any olives, could you?

[*They exit.*]

The Visit

Characters:	TOM—'Doubting Thomas' of the Gospels. JESUS
Plot:	JESUS visits TOM and takes him out into the world.
Main Point:	That Jesus goes with us to give the gospel to the world.
Running Time:	5 minutes.
Suitability:	Church event.
Staging:	Table; two chairs.
Props/Costumes:	Coats on the backs of chairs. Wine, two glasses. Plate of bread rolls.
Remarks:	JESUS should be friendly and confident. He should have some 'life' about him.

[*Enter* TOM. *He is preparing some food—an ordinary meal with some wine to accompany it. He turns to SR to pour some wine.* JESUS *enters SL and sits at the table.* TOM *turns to see him sitting there, not having noticed him enter.*]

TOM: What . . . how . . . how did you get in here?
JESUS: Door.
TOM: It's locked.
JESUS: I know. Why did you lock it? What are you afraid of?

TOM: It . . . it's dangerous these days. Who are you?

JESUS: Oh come on, Tom. You know who I am. You just don't want to believe it, that's all.

TOM: They said they'd seen you.

JESUS: Yes. They did.

TOM: [*Beginning to speak and then stopping himself*] I was going to say 'how are you?'

JESUS: Fine. Never better. Yourself?

TOM: Oh I'm fine, I'm fine. I'm talking to a dead man, why wouldn't I be fine? It's the chicken. I knew there was something wrong with the chicken.

JESUS: Is that wine?

[TOM *hands* JESUS *the glass of wine he had poured for himself*.]

TOM: Food poisoning.

JESUS: [*Laughing*] Food poisoning?

TOM: It's that butcher. Dead dodgy. All the dogs in his neighbourhood have disappeared. I should have known.

JESUS: [*Tasting wine*] That's not bad, that. I've made better of course.

TOM: Or you're a dream. A horrible dream.

JESUS: Horrible? Is it horrible to see me again?

TOM: It's horrible because it's not true. It's not real. I'm ill.

JESUS: Oh Tom! An explanation for everything, and never the right one.

TOM: [*Turning away and filling another glass of wine.*] When the others said you were back I didn't believe them. I mean sometimes when you want something badly enough, you create it for yourself—an illusion. I remember when I was young I crossed the desert, only my water bottle burst, see, and I was a long way from any water. I wanted that water! I needed it so badly. After a while I saw an oasis in the distance, all lush and green. I ran towards it and it was nothing! Just sand! I'd created it for myself you see . . .

[*He turns to see* JESUS *helping himself to the food on the table.*]

TOM: Oi! That's my dinner!

JESUS: Don't mind me. I'm just a mirage.

TOM: This is insane! Dead men do not eat. Dead men do not walk around.

JESUS: Oh yes they do. Go to the window. Look at the people walking around with their eyes closed, walking in the dark, because they have no idea who they really are. They haven't met me. They're the dead people, Tom. Needs more salt.

TOM: Look, I . . . I'm finding this rather a strain. I mean I saw you! I saw you . . . I've never had dinner with a corpse before.

JESUS: I'm not a corpse.

TOM: You were.

JESUS: So were you, before we met. This is dead good you know.

TOM: Thanks. When the others said they'd met you, I said I'd want the proof.

JESUS: Shake hands?

TOM: What?

JESUS: Well that was it, wasn't it? My hands and my feet. Come on Tom, do you really need to see the scars?

TOM: No, I know it's you. I knew the moment I saw you.

JESUS: Why did you lock the door? Were you locking yourself in, or trying to lock me out?

TOM: I didn't understand what was happening. I still don't. I mean why did you do it? What was it all for?

JESUS: It was for you Tom. I did it for you. You and all the other helpless people in the world.

TOM: Wasn't there an easier way?

JESUS: No. There wasn't an easier way.

TOM: I thought it was the end. I thought I'd never see you again, and then when the others said ... well—what's the point of building up your hopes? I didn't want to believe what they said, in case it wasn't true. [*Emotionally*] All my life I've lost things! When I was young, I loved animals—people used to bring them to me to look after: birds with broken wings, injured dogs—and I would help them. Cure them. And if they recovered they'd go back into the wild. I'd lose them. I mean you pour all your love into them and then you lose them! [*Quietly*] And that's what I thought had happened to you.

JESUS: I know. Do you think I don't know that? Because I've done it, Tom. I've poured myself out for millions of people—injured, hurt people who won't ever care, won't ever love me back. But also for some who will. I'm back, Tom. I'm back for good. Did you really think you'd lost me?

TOM: I dunno. You used to talk in riddles so much.

JESUS: [*Affectionately*] Thicko.

TOM: I know. But you're the Son of God, I'm just another man.

JESUS: No-one is 'just another man' to me, Tom.

TOM: And you're back?

JESUS: For keeps. They couldn't hold me, Tom, not the nails or the cross, or the powers of hell itself! Nothing could hold me. But you can, if you want.

[*He picks up* TOM*'s coat from the chair and hands it to him.*]

JESUS: Come on. Open the door. Let's go together and tell all the unreal people. Let's go and bring life to the dead.

TOM: Together?

JESUS: Together.

[*They exit.*]

Conversing with the Dumb

by Roger Porthouse

Characters:	SHARON—East London teenager. Slightly tarty. She works in a loo roll factory. GOD —The caring mentor. Fun-loving, but keen for his pupils to learn.
Plot:	Prayer time on five successive days in Sharon's bedsit.
Main Point:	Prayer is a two way link. Not just a time for you to speak to God, but also for God to speak to you.
Running Time:	Approx 8 minutes.
Suitability:	Christian event.
Staging:	A drab bedsit in London. Door SL with bed R of CS. Chair is DSC and an imaginary window is SL. USC sits God on his throne [*raised platform*].
Props/Costumes:	Bed, chair, handbag, mirror, lipstick, tissue, coat, bag of shopping.

[*Enter* SHARON. *She goes over to the bed and kneels to pray. Pauses, opens handbag, checks face in mirror. Satisfied, resumes praying position.*]

SHARON: [*In loud, proclaiming voice*] Oh Lord . . .
GOD: Yes.

SHARON: [*Slow and deliberate punctuation*] I cometh before thee as a wicked transgressor of thy perfect law . . .

GOD: Oh dear. [*Looking over his shoulder*] Gabriel, can you bring me the old English translation books . . . Yes, another one . . . no, Sharon . . . that's right, Thursday, last week. Mission to Walthamstow.

SHARON: Forgiveth me of my iniquities [*pronounced in-ick-quee-itys*] and leadev . . . leadef . . . er . . . leadeth me in thy everlasting ways! [*Giving up and going back to E. London*] Aoww Gawd! Do I 'ave to use that old stuff?

GOD: Gabriel, forget it, I think we're getting somewhere. [*To* SHARON] No Sharon, of course not.

SHARON: I mean, it gets right up your nose after a while, an' I get confused wiv wot I'm sayin'.

[*She sits on the bed in a huff.*]

GOD: So do I, Sharon, so do I.

SHARON: Look, it's no good. I'll have to think this out. I'll try again tomorrow.

[*Picks up bag and moves to door.*]

GOD: Hang on Sharon, I want to talk to . . .

[*Exit* SHARON.]

GOD: . . . you.

[*Blackout. Lights up. Enter* SHARON *hurried and excited. She throws her coat down and kneels by the bed, eyes closed.*]

SHARON: Dear God.

GOD: Hi, Sharon.

SHARON: I've got some really good news for you!

GOD: [*Surprised*] Really?

SHARON: I wos talkin' to Sue during tea break—she's me shift leader . . . the one who took me to Walthamstow . . . anyway, we wos 'avin' a chat, like yer do, an' she said I don't 'ave to use all that Shakespeare stuff when I pray to you!

GOD: [*Relieved*] Oh good. I'm glad she passed the message on.

SHARON: Well, I said that's great, innit? An' she said I could talk to you as if you wos me friend!

GOD: [*Taken aback*] I am your friend!

SHARON: As yer can imagine, this solves a lot of problems wiv the 'thees' and 'thous' an' 'holy art thy's'.

[GOD *gives a slightly puzzled look.*]

SHARON: Anyhow. She said I should speak to yer as if I wos talkin' to someone on the phone . . .

GOD: [*Wanting to come down*] Great! So can I . . .

SHARON: Now . . .

[GOD *sighs.*]

SHARON: If we're goin' to be friends, you better call me Shaz, it's short for Sharon.

GOD: You surprise me.

SHARON: And if you don't mind, I'll call you Jesus . . .

GOD: Sharon . . .

SHARON: [*Thinking*] Well, I could call you Jesus . . .

GOD: Shaz . . .

SHARON: But then again, God is kinda catchy!

GOD: You're not listening to me, are you?

SHARON: Tell yer wot.

GOD: [*Mimicking*] Wot?

SHARON: I'll swop between the two! God one day an' Jesus the next! All right?

GOD: Fine, but can I . . .

SHARON: Ooooh, I almost forgot. God bless Mum an' God . . . [*stops, thinks, and grins*] Jesus bless Dad. Amen.

[*She gets up and moves to the door.*]

GOD: I'd love to. Now, can I say some . . .

[*Exit* SHARON.]

GOD: ... thing!

[GOD *stops, looks around earth, below, to L.*]

GOD: Sue ...

[*Blackout. Lights up, as* SHARON *enters confidently. Puts shopping bag down and leans against chair.*]

GOD: Ah! Shaz, I've been ...

SHARON: Hi God! [*Checks herself*] Or is it Jesus today? Oh wot the he ... [*Splutters*] He—he—heck! Yer know what I mean. [*Strolling around*] I've learnt something new today!

GOD: I can see.

SHARON: In case yer 'aven't noticed, I'm not on me knees, an' me eyes are open!

GOD: I noticed.

SHARON: It's not outa disrespect, mind yer. No, don't get me wrong!

GOD: Could I?

SHARON: It's just that I wos told I can talk to yer anyway I want. As long as it's not [*slowly*] dir-rog-gat-tree.

GOD: Yes, and I can talk to you in all sorts of ways if you'd only ...

SHARON: Yer see, praying's about us 'aving a chat and although I can talk to yer wiv me eyes shut, [*shuts eyes tightly*] like this, I can also talk to yer wiv me eyes open, [*opens eyes wide*] like this! [*Frown*] But yer see there's a little problem there. If you an' me are meant to be 'aving a chat, why do I do all the chattin'?

GOD: [*Mimicking*] 'Cos yer never stop to listen!

SHARON: Sue said prayer wos a two way thing, like conversation ...

GOD: It is, it is.

SHARON: So, God, I wos wonderin' whether you could chat back sometimes ...

GOD: I have done, but you haven't noticed!

SHARON: Right. I think that's about all for now. Amen.
[*She nods in confirmation. Blackout. Lights up.*]

SHARON: I'm home, God!

GOD: I would never have guessed.

SHARON: [*Humble*] First things first. I'm sorry about wot I said to Pauline. It just slipped out.

GOD: That's okay.

SHARON: [*Proud*] I've learnt three new things today! [*Getting mirror and lipstick out*] One: I found out that not only can I talk to yer wiv me eyes open, but [*muffled voice while she puts lipstick on*] while I'm doin' other things as well.
[*Takes away mirror to reveal lipstick around her face. Looks back into mirror.*]

SHARON: Aooowww!
[*Disgruntled, she wipes face with tissue.* GOD *finds this amusing.*]

SHARON: I 'aven't quite got the knack of it yet. Where wos I? Oh yeah . . . second: I don't 'ave to talk out loud. I can talk to yer in me [*points to head while she concentrates*] if I want to. An' thirdly, I can talk to yer at work as well as home . . .

GOD: Get away!

SHARON: In fact, I can talk to you any time I like, wherever I am an' wotever I'm doing!

GOD: You can listen as well if you'd only stop . . .

SHARON: Oooh, I almost forgot to tell you . . .
[GOD *gives a heavy sigh.*]

SHARON: I got promotion! I used to be chief counter of the blue an' red loo rolls; you know, makin' sure each roll 'ad two 'undred sheets . . . anyhow, I bet you can't guess wot I do now . . .

GOD: [*Dull*] Junior perforator.

SHARON: Junior perforator!

GOD: [*Mock surprise*] Oh! What a surprise!

SHARON: I put the little holes in the sheets so yer can tear them off more easily!

GOD: You told me.

SHARON: In case yer don't remember, I told yer that at work. [*More humble*] I'm only on the paper ones at the moment. [*Enthusiastic*] But it won't be long before I'm back on the tissues!

GOD: Well, I wouldn't worry much about th . . .

SHARON: Which brings me to another point. On Sunday, the vicar said that 'we', as in the congrigestion, should praise you by the way we work . . . and . . . well [*lowly*] it's a bit difficult when you're just putting 'oles in loo paper. [*Cheerful*] Any'ow, won't go on. I'm sure you've other things to do. Jesus bless Mum 'n God bless Dad. Amen.

GOD: Ah well, time for a change of tack. [*Looks down at earth again*] Ah! Sue, how's Sharon getting on . . ?

[*Blackout. Lights up as* SHARON *is entering, half-way through a conversation with God.*]

SHARON: An' then we both had a chat to you wiv our eyes shut. Remember . . ?

GOD: Yes, I remember.

SHARON: I always knew the Bible wos wot yer said in the past, but I didn't know it's wot yer sayin' today. [*Ponders*] That's clever that is! Speakin' to different people wiv the same book.

GOD: But that's not the only way I speak to peo . . .

SHARON: But that's not the only way you speak to people. Sue wos telling me that you speak through other people too. Like the vicar on Sunday, when 'e's in 'is pullypit and through [*realisation*] 'ere . . . 'ang on a mo. You speak through others too! You little tinker, you!

GOD: Really . . .

SHARON: You wos speakin' to me through Sue weren't you?

GOD: [*Happy*] Shaz . . .

SHARON: To think that all the time, me askin' you all them questions an' yer giving me the answers through someone else . . .

GOD: Shaz, slow down.

SHARON: An' I didn't even realise . . . ooooh, that's stopped me in me tracks, that 'as!

[SHARON *sits on the bed.*]

GOD: Listen.

SHARON: [*Plea*] Will yer speak through me . . .

GOD: [*Loving*] I'll speak *to* you!

SHARON: Or do you just speak through shift leaders and vicars?

GOD: Look outside.

SHARON: I wonder . . .

[*She goes and looks out of the window.*]

SHARON: Oooh, the stars. [*Dreamily*] I like the stars.

GOD: See my creation.

SHARON: [*Reciting*] In the beginning, God created the 'eavens an' the earth . . .

[GOD *comes down from throne and stands behind* SHARON.]

SHARON: You made them all, didn't ya . . ?

GOD: Yes.

SHARON: You ain't 'alf clever, God!

[*She moves to the bed.*]

GOD: Thanks. [*Turning to* SHARON, *staying still*] I put . . .

SHARON: You put them stars there so we can see the power of your creation.

GOD: You're learning!

[SHARON *gets into bed.*]

SHARON: Just think of all them stars an' planets an' things . . . an' little me.

GOD: I love you.

SHARON: It makes me feel all cared for an' loved . . . [*she ponders on the thought*] It is, innit?

GOD: What?

SHARON: It's another one of your ways of speaking to me! I use a phone, an' you use a video-thingummyjig!

GOD: That's one way of looking at it.

SHARON: An' I used to think that prayin' wos about me talkin' an you just listenin' . . . it's a bit of a shock really.

GOD: What's the point in talking to me if you don't expect me to answer . . ?

SHARON: I suppose it's only natural for yer to want to talk back. [*Getting sleepy*] It's funny, really, 'ere wos I askin' yer to chat back, an' when yer did, I didn't even realise . . .

GOD: [*Coming across to bed*] I always talk back, but you have to learn the ways to listen.

[SHARON *goes to sleep.*]

GOD: [*Loving, quiet, paternal*] Thank you for listening. Keep listening.

[*He places his hand on her head, as if blessing.*]

GOD: Goodnight, Shaz . . .

[*He collects chair from CS and brings it over beside the bed. He sits on it, and watches over* SHARON. *Lights fade to darkness.*]

Injury Time

Characters:	ONE and TWO are both football supporters of the yob type.
Plot:	Two men watch the crucifixion as if it were some kind of sporting event.
Main Point:	That people did go to these kinds of things for entertainment and that Jesus was someone out of the ordinary.
Running Time:	5 minutes.
Suitability:	Church event.
Staging:	Minimal room needed.
Props/Costumes:	ONE and TWO wear leather jackets and football scarves. If you want to go the whole hog they can wear Doc Martin's as well.
Remarks:	This is a loud, aggressive piece. The actors need to have that aggressive, threatening, mocking edge to their voice when they shout. Gestures and the direction they are looking and shouting should indicate where the action is taking place.

[*Enter* ONE *and* TWO. *They are two typical football yobs.*]

BOTH: [*Singing*] 'Ere we go! 'Ere we go! 'Ere we go . . .

ONE: Oh—this is it—we're into injury time!

[*They pause momentarily and watch the action.*]

TWO: Our lot are a bit slow today.

ONE: Yeah, looking forward to their day off I expect. Come on you lot—get a move on! The holiday doesn't start till tomorrow!

TWO: Look at them! They're normally much more organised than this . . . running around like headless chickens! I thought you lot were supposed to be a team! A trained unit!

ONE: Hang on, they've got their act together now . . . they've got that one on the right at full stretch.

[*They cheer.*]

TWO: Nice move!

ONE: That's one at any rate! Ooohhh look at his face! He's not happy about that!

TWO: Here we go, 'ere we go . . . oh look, our lot are all over them now. Here we go and . . . wham! That's two!

ONE: This is more like it. This is what I came to see! Teamwork!

TWO: What's the matter—did it go straight through your hands?

ONE: That was good to watch.

TWO: Yeah well, it's that new boy, just come in from Italy. Touch of continental skill. One of the best strikers in the business.

ONE: Look, look they're off again! Come on lads . . .

[*They cheer.*]

ONE: Driven home!

TWO: Brilliant stuff! That's three in two minutes!

ONE: That's taken all the stuffing out of them! [*Looking up to Jesus on the cross*] No use looking like that, mate—if you'd defended yourself better you wouldn't be in this position.

TWO: That looks about it.

ONE: Yeah, it's all over now.

TWO: Bit disappointed in the opposition. They didn't put up much of a struggle. Look at 'em now—heads down, just hanging around. Come on, keep moving! Give us a bit of entertainment!

ONE: Load of wimps. Look at that one at the back. Call that a body? I've seen more muscular pipecleaners!

TWO: Ah look, he's thirsty! He's worn out! What's the matter—can't take the pace? And I thought he was supposed to be the star!

ONE: Yeah well, it's all reputation innit? All talk of what he's going to do, but come the big day he's just not up to it!

TWO: Tell you what—let's go and see if we can find some of their supporters afterwards and give 'em a good going over!

ONE: Yeah, should be easy pickings!

TWO: Still, bit of an anticlimax really, wasn't it? I was expecting more of a struggle . . . I don't like the way he looks at you.

ONE: Who?

TWO: The one at the back. Golden boy. The way he looked at me then, like it wasn't the end . . .

ONE: Well it soon will be.

TWO: No, it's strange . . . look at him! There's something about him. He thinks he's won!

ONE: Well he's wrong! No good looking like that mate! This is it! You're dead and buried with no chance of a replay!

TWO: Strange bloke. What was his name again?

ONE: Jesus. Take no notice. He's a born loser! Once those Romans got their act together he was finished. Three of 'em nailed up just like that! Good old fashioned entertainment.

ONE: Look at him just hanging there! No attempt to fight back. He's not a real criminal at all.

TWO: No, he's just been sent on as a substitute.

ONE: Ah well, might as well go then.

[*They start to exit, slowly. After a pause,* ONE *looks about him.*]

TWO: Dark innit?

[*They exit.*]

Ordering the Food

Characters: SHOPKEEPER
WOMAN

Plot: A woman is buying her food for Christmas.

Main Point: Er . . . pass.

Running Time: 5 minutes.

Suitability: Christmas performance.

Staging: Shop counter.

Props/Costumes: Apron for SHOPKEEPER, long list for WOMAN.

[*Enter* WOMAN.]

WOMAN: Hello? [*Yells*] Shop!

[SHOPKEEPER *rises from behind the counter, slightly deafened.*]

SHOPKEEPER: Hello, madam, what can I do for you?

WOMAN: Oh. I have a list here.

[*Pulls out list which at first looks to be a single sheet of paper, but which drops open to a huge length.*]

WOMAN: Now, off-licence first. I want 3 crates of Newcastle Brown Ale; 2 crates of Guinness; 5 bottles of whisky; a quart of vodka; 3 pints of Bull's Blood; 3 bottles of dry Martini. [*Pause*] A barrel of dry cider; 6 bottles of gin; a crate of tonic water and a bottle of meths for Daddy.

SHOPKEEPER: [*Taken aback*] Having a party?

WOMAN: [*Sarcastically*] No, the Vicar's coming for the evening. Of course we're having a party! It's Christmas isn't it? You've got to enter into the spirit of the thing.

SHOPKEEPER: Sounds more like you're going to drown in the spirit of the thing. Drink a lot your family?

WOMAN: Always have. I remember Grandad's cremation. You could see the blaze across three counties. Now, I shall want a bird of course.

SHOPKEEPER: Of course.

WOMAN: A small one should suffice. About fifty pounds.

SHOPKEEPER: Pardon?

WOMAN: Fifty pounds.

SHOPKEEPER: You don't want a turkey—you want an ostrich!

WOMAN: [*Pause*] Yes, that would be nice. It's been a long time since we had an ostrich.

SHOPKEEPER: You actually want one?

WOMAN: Oh yes—and I think a joint for Boxing Day as well. A nice leg of hippo, or best end of aardvark. Although who can say which is actually the best end of aardvarks?

SHOPKEEPER: Quite. Er . . . do you eat hippo a lot?

WOMAN: Great heavens no! I mean—it's Christmas isn't it? You've got to have something special. Good Lord, they don't get aardvark every day you know. Most days they have to make do with plain old scrag end of lamb, or roast parrot.

SHOPKEEPER: Parrot?

WOMAN: So economical don't you think?

SHOPKEEPER: Well I'm sorry madam, we don't sell ostrich.

WOMAN: Don't sell ostrich?

SHOPKEEPER: No. Nor indeed, aardvark.

WOMAN: But Christmas wouldn't be Christmas without aardvark!

SHOPKEEPER: I'm very sorry.

WOMAN: Well, it'll have to be something else then. How about wildebeest?

SHOPKEEPER: Er . . . no.

WOMAN: Three-toed sloth?

SHOPKEEPER: Sorry?

WOMAN: Coypu? Springbok? Dugong? Kermodes Bear? Huntingdon's Pole Cat?

SHOPKEEPER: 'Fraid not.

WOMAN: Not very well stocked are you? What *have* you got?

SHOPKEEPER: We've got some turkey.

WOMAN: We don't eat turkey.

SHOPKEEPER: But everyone eats turkey for Christmas!

WOMAN: Well, we don't.

SHOPKEEPER: Well, I can't help you madam.

WOMAN: Oh dash it! I suppose it's off to Harrods again.

SHOPKEEPER: Is that where you usually go?

WOMAN: No, normally we go to the zoo, but they've raised the fences this year. Anyway, it's never easy smuggling an ostrich out in a plastic bag.

[*She turns to leave, but stops abruptly.*]

WOMAN: Wait a minute—I'll have that!

SHOPKEEPER: What?

WOMAN: [*Points*] That!

SHOPKEEPER: But you can't . . .

WOMAN: I won't take no for an answer.

SHOPKEEPER: But . . .

WOMAN: Have it delivered.

[*She exits.* SHOPKEEPER *looks bewildered. Shouts, off.*]

SHOPKEEPER: Ethel! I've got a bit of a problem! I've just sold next door's cat!

[*Exits.*]

LESSON FIVE
SERIES

The following sketches are a group of six. I will leave it to the author to describe them in detail, but I think it worth a few words on the subject of series.

The main difference between series and one-off plays is the fact that series keep on going. That may seem obvious to you, but, as dear, dear Dame Peggy once said to me, 'Stating the obvious is what makes you the great teacher you are.' Of course, she wasn't Dame Peggy then, she was actually Major General Ernest Bleckington, but that's another story.

Series, as we have pointed out, keep on going. That means that you will play the same character twice, thrice, maybe even fource. Therefore don't start the series with a ridiculous accent or strange limp, as you will have to keep it going in every subsequent appearance.

I have considerable experience in this area. Four years of my career were spent playing the part of 'Daisy' in the Archers. It was a taxing part—each episode I had to 'moo' whilst being milked by Doris. Of course, one gets terribly attached to a character like that, and I felt a real sense of bereavement when, after three successful calvings, Daisy caught bovine TB and died. But that's showbusiness.

The Acts of Ludicrus

Introduction: *The Acts of Ludicrus* was written for Spring Harvest, as a 'soap opera' to complement the morning Bible studies. As such it proved very popular and very effective (the cleaners, who came in before the morning session to prepare the venue, used to stay on to watch it as they got 'hooked' by the story). In six episodes, it tells the story of a family in Judea at the time of the book of Acts. The series revolves around LUDICRUS, the slave and the household he works for. Certain characters therefore, appear in all or most of the episodes and these are listed below. Other characters are listed at the head of each episode.

Characters:

ANNOUNCER—on Radio Judea.

LUDICRUS—a slave.

GORILLA GASTROENTERITIS—his mistress.

MAXIMUS GASTROENTERITIS—his master, a minor official in the Roman government.

	POMPUS HIPPOPOTAMUS—a centurion, and brother of Gorilla.
	VANILLA GASTROENTERITIS—their daughter and an early Christian.
	THE RUBBER CHICKEN—non-speaking part.
Running Time:	Each episode lasts approximately 10 minutes.
Suitability:	Any event that allows you six ten-minute slots, e.g. a Mission, or church weekend.
Staging:	Four chairs forming a Roman couch for characters to recline on CS.
Props/Costumes:	Most importantly, LUDICRUS has a RUBBER CHICKEN which is his constant companion. Characters wear togas, robes, sandalled feet. Centurion POMPUS wears a tiny Roman helmet which perches on the top of his head and carries a sword. MAXIMUS has a briefcase.
Remarks:	Each sketch in the series starts with a radio jingle and announcement. The jingle should be sung à la Radio One, and the day's news read over some suitably innocuous backing music. These are optional, but if you can include them they give a very good start to each episode.

EPISODE ONE

Plot: VANILLA has become a Christian and has sold her jewellery to help the poor. This causes problems for LUDICRUS who is accused of theft.

Main Point: Christianity costs. It means a break with the old life.

Props/Costumes: LUDICRUS has a broom and, of course, the RUBBER CHICKEN. POMPUS has his sword.

JINGLE: 'Friends, Romans, Countrymen, lend us your ears . . .'

ANNOUNCER: [*Offstage, through microphone, over backing music.*]
Hi, everybody out there in radio land! This is Radio Judea saying a big good morning to all Romans, Jews, Greeks, Assyrians, Egyptians, Samarians and Welsh! We start this morning with some traffic news—the C25 chariot way has been closed at Junction 17, that's the Tyre and Sidon turn off, because a large elephant has shed its load. Drivers are recommended to find an alternative route. The weather in Jerusalem and the surrounding areas will be dry and

dusty, as it has been for the past thirty-seven years . . .

[*Enter* LUDICRUS, *sweeping the floor. He doesn't notice the audience at first.*]

LUDICRUS: [*Singing*] Ole Man Tiber, dat ole man Tiber, he must know sumpin' but he don't . . . oh, excuse me. I didn't realise we had visitors. Welcome, oh illustrious ones to Duodenum, a small suburb of Jerusalem. Allow me to introduce myself—I am Ludicrus, slave to Maximus Gastroenteritis and his wife the lovely Mistress Gorilla. Yes—a slave! Lowest of the low! Downtrodden! Repressed! At everyone's beck and call! Oh misery! Oh woe is me! Ill-treated and abused! At the mercy of a cruel and heartless master . . .

[GORILLA *has entered SL, behind him.*]

GORILLA: Have you quite finished?

LUDICRUS: Oh mistress, I didn't see you there. Here, come and recline. [*To audience*] This is my mistress Gorilla. Looks like she's had a bad night. [*To* GORILLA] Did you sleep well, mistress?

GORILLA: No. I went to next door's house-warming orgy. Oh my head!

[LUDICRUS *guides her to the couch.*]

LUDICRUS: Let me get you a cup of wine.

GORILLA: Oh no, not more wine! Hasn't this country got anything but wine?

LUDICRUS: There's water.

GORILLA Water! At least the wine's healthy.

LUDICRUS: Well, how about this new drink they're all talking about, the one that's imported from India. You get the leaves of a bush, dry them and then crush them up, then you pour boiling water on them, add some goat's milk and sugar and drink it.

GORILLA: I think I'm going to throw up.

[*Enter* MAXIMUS *SL.*]

MAXIMUS: Morning dear.

LUDICRUS: Morning.

MAXIMUS: I didn't mean you, slave.

LUDICRUS: [*To audience*] Charming isn't he? This is Maximus Gastroenteritis, my master and minor official in the Roman government of occupation here in Judea.

MAXIMUS: This is an exciting day for me, you know. I'm chairing the new Judean sewage sub-committee.

LUDICRUS: Such excitement.

GORILLA: 'Sewage' did you say?

LUDICRUS: Yes, honestly, this country—they just throw it out of the windows onto the streets, so you have to walk through it. It's disgusting. Some days you can see what people have been eating.

[GORILLA *throws up, behind the couch.*]

MAXIMUS: Not feeling well, dear?

GORILLA: It was that party last night.

LUDICRUS: We have new neighbours then, master?

MAXIMUS: Yes, that chap Joseph sold up and left. Got involved with some loony sect apparently. The new people are Mr and Mrs Bulbus from Rome. They're debauched, rich, and they hold loud orgies every weekend. Just the kind of neighbours we needed! Well, duty calls. The sewage sub-committee awaits.

GORILLA: Thrilling.

MAXIMUS: You can scoff, but it's very important, there's a lot of work to be done. I may have to bring some of my work home with me.

GORILLA: Oh, have you seen Vanilla?

MAXIMUS: No.

LUDICRUS: She went out early this morning, mistress.

GORILLA: Again? I don't know where she gets to. Only I wanted to borrow her gold chain, you know, the one she keeps in the little cabinet by her bed.

MAXIMUS: I'm sure she won't mind. Well, goodbye my precious sweet.

GORILLA: Goodbye.

MAXIMUS: Don't I get a little kissy-wissy?

GORILLA: [*Evidently not feeling up to it*] Oh—Ludicrus.

LUDICRUS: Really! The things we slaves have to do!

[LUDICRUS *kisses his master.* GORILLA *and* MAXIMUS *exit SR.* LUDICRUS *crosses behind the couch and puts on an apron. He pickes up the* RUBBER CHICKEN *and sits down on the couch, preparing it for lunch.*]

LUDICRUS: [*To audience*] I'm preparing lunch. Roast goat's entrails and stuffed sparrows' tongues marinated in vinegar. On toast. Oh—and this chicken. Now—Vanilla, whom you heard mentioned this morning, she is the daughter of the household. She's joined this sect you see—she's become one of these Christians. And every morning at the crack of dawn, she goes out to join with them in prayers. Yes—she's a very early Christian.

[*Fanfare. Enter* POMPUS *SR.*]

LUDICRUS: [*To audience*] Oh, just what I needed. This is the mistress's brother—he's a centurion. And a right pain in the legionaries.

POMPUS: Hail!

LUDICRUS: Looks all right to me.

POMPUS: Slave! Centurion Pompus Hippopotamus is here!

LUDICRUS: Whoopee.

POMPUS: Well grovel then.

LUDICRUS: Oh grovel, grovel, grovel.

POMPUS: That's enough. Where's your mistress?

LUDICRUS: I have no idea, oh mighty one. [*To audience*] Gone out shopping I expect. Really—the sestertii that woman gets through! [*To* POMPUS] She's probably trying on togas in Marcus et Spencerius. Now, if you'll excuse me, I've got to stuff this chicken.

[*He begins to stuff the* CHICKEN. *As he does so there is a scream from offstage.*]

LUDICRUS: [*To* CHICKEN] Oh sorry, were my hands cold?

GORILLA: [*Offstage*] Theft! Theft!

[*Enter* GORILLA *SL. She rushes across to* POMPUS *SR.*]

POMPUS: Gorilla! What is it?

GORILLA: Oh Pompus, I'm so glad you're here! There's been a burglary!

POMPUS: A burglary?

GORILLA: They've stolen some jewellery!

POMPUS: Jewellery?

GORILLA: Vanilla's gold chain!

POMPUS: Gold?

GORILLA: What are you—a parrot?

POMPUS: Parrot? Oh I see. Well, anyway, I'll take over. Someone call the police.

GORILLA: Pompus—you *are* the police.

POMPUS: Oh yes. Well, what exactly has happened?

GORILLA: Vanilla's gold chain has disappeared. I was going to wear it this morning. Ludicrus heard me say where it was kept . . .

POMPUS: Really?

[*They both look at* LUDICRUS *with suspicion.*]

LUDICRUS: [*Trying to hide*] There's nobody here but us chickens!

POMPUS: [*Chasing* LUDICRUS *round the couch*] Slave! Where have you put the gold?

LUDICRUS: Gold? I haven't got any gold! Why would I want to wear jewellery? My reputation's bad enough after having to kiss the master each morning! I'm innocent!

GORILLA: You've sold it!

POMPUS: Please Gorilla, let me handle this. It needs a bit of psychology.

[POMPUS *draws his sword.*]

LUDICRUS: What are you doing?

POMPUS: I'm going to cut your head off unless you tell me where the gold is.

LUDICRUS: Great psychology.

POMPUS: Now are you going to admit it, or are you going to watch your head roll across the floor?

LUDICRUS: Don't I get a third choice?

POMPUS: Right, here we go!

LUDICRUS: I'm innocent! Innocent! Look—I'm stuffing a chicken—you wouldn't kill a man wearing a chicken would you?

POMPUS: Prepare to die!

[LUDICRUS *falls to the ground and grovels,* POMPUS *stands over him about to behead him. Enter* VANILLA *SR.*]

VANILLA: Hello everybody! What are you doing down there, Ludicrus?

LUDICRUS: Grovelling, mistress. I'm about to be filleted.

POMPUS: He stole your gold chain!

VANILLA: Oh Uncle Pompus don't be so silly. I sold it.

GORILLA: You sold it?

VANILLA: Yes.

GORILLA: You sold your gold?

VANILLA: I gave the money to the poor—to some old people. They needed warm clothing.

GORILLA: You sold your gold for the cold old?

POMPUS: Why?

VANILLA: Jesus told me to. It's my new friends you see. We meet together and pray and read the scriptures and we share everything. I'm a Christian.

GORILLA: Does your father know about this?

VANILLA: I shouldn't think so. I haven't told anyone yet. Except Ludicrus.

GORILLA: Ludicrus? You knew?

LUDICRUS: I'd forgotten. It had completely slipped my mind!

GORILLA: But you can't be serious!

VANILLA: Of course I am.

POMPUS: [*Waving sword around*] Let me try some psychology on her . . .

[GORILLA *pushes* POMPUS *away to SR.*]

GORILLA: No, no, no, let me handle this. Vanilla! Think of the family. Think of your father.

VANILLA: There's nothing you can say.

POMPUS: But these Christian chappies! They're a bunch of revolutionaries. Undermining the state. I mean surely you can't turn your back on your Roman lifestyle—all the good things you've got?

VANILLA: Name one.

POMPUS: Well there's ... er ... orgies! They're good aren't they? I mean, I'm all for a bit of morality providing it doesn't interfere with the orgies.

VANILLA: But that's just it. If what I believe is true then it has to interfere. I'm serious about this, Mummy. I'm going to sell what I own and share it with others.

[VANILLA *and* GORILLA *sit on the couch.*]

VANILLA: I'm going to try and live out what I believe. I'm going to sell my gold and silver and my purple toga, all the stuff I wear to parties and that I don't really need. The poor can have it.

GORILLA: Don't be silly dear. What would they do with it? The poor don't get invited to any parties. Oh! I'd better call your father home from the office! And him with all his sewage on his hands! I'm sure it's only a phase ...

VANILLA: You really don't understand do you?

[VANILLA *exits SR.*]

GORILLA: [*To* LUDICRUS] And I'll deal with you later.

POMPUS: Please let me try some psychology on her ...

[GORILLA *and* POMPUS *exit SR.*]

LUDICRUS: What have I done? I'm just trying to stuff a chicken! [*To audience*] Well, there we are. As you can see, life here is never dull. Boring, yes, but never dull. I don't know about this Christianity. I mean, they're all so different, aren't they? Of course the time may come when you can't tell the difference between the Christians and the non-believers. Ah

well, we'll leave it there for now, shall we? So, for the moment, from the chicken and myself—farewell.
[*Exits.*]

EPISODE TWO

Extra Characters: VOICES 1, 2 and 3—offstage in the market place.
MYOPIA—an ex-blind beggar.
A visiting VIP (non-speaking part)

Plot: LUDICRUS is detailed to keep VANILLA out of trouble. This he fails to do. She goes to the market place, heals a beggar and gets thrown into prison. Then she escapes during an earthquake.

Main Point: The early Christians were ordinary, but achieved some extra-ordinary things.

Staging: The chairs are rearranged halfway through this episode to form a line SL which represents a wall out of the prison. When she escapes, VANILLA should clamber through these.

Props/Costumes: Newspaper and begging bowl for MYOPIA.

Remarks: The VIP is best played by someone well-known to the audience, but who doesn't know what's going on. It's a non-speaking part, all he/she has to do is stand there. Don't tell them anything in advance and it will increase the comic effect during the 'earthquake' when LUDICRUS and MAXIMUS are rushing about, and the VIP is just standng there, looking bemused.

JINGLE: 'Friends, Romans, Countrymen, lend us your ears . . .'

ANNOUNCER: Hi and welcome to you again, from Radio Judea, broadcasting to you live throughout the Middle East. Roman Governor, Pontius Pilate was at the centre of a demonstration by Jewish activists today. As he opened a new bridge he was pelted with eggs. Said Pilate, 'I wouldn't have minded, but the eggs were still inside the chickens.' Today's weather? Dry and dusty, as usual.

[*Enter* LUDICRUS, *holding* CHICKEN.]

LUDICRUS: Well now, if you remember, yesterday we saw how young Vanilla, daughter of Maximus Gastroenteritis had become one of those new-fangled Christians, how she'd sold all her gold for the cold old and how my attempts to stuff this chicken were hindered by a death threat thinly disguised as psychology. Still with me? Of course, at that time her father hadn't heard about the situation, but Gorilla Gastroenteritis, my mistress, has just called her husband home from work and Vanilla is just telling him the news. Excuse me . . .

[LUDICRUS *eavesdrops*.]

MAXIMUS: [*Offstage*] Noooooooooooooooo!!!!!

LUDICRUS: Well, I think he's taken that very well, don't you?

[*Enter* MAXIMUS.]

MAXIMUS: [*Frantically*] My own daughter! My own daughter!

LUDICRUS: Something wrong master?

MAXIMUS: My own daughter, Ludicrus, my own daughter!

LUDICRUS: So you said. Here—sit down. Take the weight off your repetitions.

[*Sits* MAXIMUS *down on couch.*]

MAXIMUS: You don't understand. She's become one of these 'Jesusians'.

LUDICRUS: They call themselves Christians.

MAXIMUS: Christians, Jesusians, same thing.

LUDICRUS: Well, I can't see it can do much harm, master.

MAXIMUS: Oh no? Think of it. Me—a high ranking official in the Roman government and my daughter has joined the enemy! Following a man who was a subversive traitor! I'll be a laughing stock! I could get thrown off the sewage sub-committee! I could get the sack! I could get ulcers and a heart attack and die in a painful horrific way with all my skin shrivelling up and my innards bursting out of me!

LUDICRUS: Yes, well, I think you're overreacting a bit, don't you?

MAXIMUS: Oh it's easy for you. You're just a slave. You don't have the weight of government on your shoulders.

LUDICRUS: Oh listen to Julius Caesar.

MAXIMUS: Look Ludicrus, you're young . . . sort of. You understand these things. You have a word with her, eh? Sort it out. Perhaps it would be best if you kept close to her over the next few days, see that she doesn't get into trouble.

LUDICRUS: Well, I don't know, I've still got this chicken to stuff . . .

MAXIMUS: It wasn't a question actually. And, of course, if anything should go wrong, then my brother-in-law would be delighted to use some of his psychology on you.

LUDICRUS: Ah.

MAXIMUS: [*Arising*] Good. Well, I feel better for having sorted that one out. Now, I've got to get back to work. I'm showing an important official from NATO round the prison this afternoon.

LUDICRUS: NATO?

MAXIMUS: North Assyrian Torturers' Organisation. Where's Gorilla?

LUDICRUS: She's gone out shopping to calm herself down.

MAXIMUS: Good grief! Does she think I'm made of sestertii? Oh well, you'll have to do. Goodbye sweetie-pie.

LUDICRUS: Oh good grief! [*Kisses him*] He hasn't even shaved.

[*Exit* MAXIMUS *SL. Enter* VANILLA *SR, upset.*]

LUDICRUS: Mistress Vanilla, what is it? What's wrong?

VANILLA: Oh, you wouldn't understand!

LUDICRUS: Try me.

VANILLA: Pictoribus atque poetis quidlibet audendi semper fit aequa potestas et hanc veniam . . .

LUDICRUS: No, not in Latin.

VANILLA: Oh, it's just everybody! They're all against me!

LUDICRUS: You're young, mistress. They think you don't know what you're doing.

VANILLA: But it's real. Why can't they accept it? Look Ludicrus, you're old. Can't you talk to them about it? Get them to understand?

LUDICRUS: I am not old. I'm only XXVIII!

VANILLA: I knew you'd do it. You're such a sweetie.

[*Enter* GORILLA *SL.*]

GORILLA: Oh there you are, Ludicrus. Has the master gone?

LUDICRUS: Yes, you just missed him.

GORILLA: Phew. I thought I might have to kiss him goodbye for a minute.

[GORILLA *sits on the couch.*]

GORILLA: Oh Vanilla. Vanilla darling, could you do Mummy a teensy-weensy, itsy-bitsy ickle favour?

VANILLA: [*Crossing and sitting next to* GORILLA] Anything Mummy.

GORILLA: Would you stop being a Christian please? Only it's upsetting your father.

VANILLA: I can't help it! I have to believe what I know to be true. You don't understand—three days ago my life changed. I can't ignore that, Mummy!

GORILLA: But think of us! Think of your parents. They'll laugh at Daddy behind his back.

VANILLA: They already laugh at him in front of his back.

GORILLA: Yes, but now they'll laugh at him all round! I mean you wouldn't want to be laughed at in stereo would you?

VANILLA: I'm sorry, Mummy. There are some things more important in life.

GORILLA: Oh I give up. Ludicrus, you deal with her.

[GORILLA *gets up and exits SL.*]

LUDICRUS: I'm confused. I can't remember who I'm persuading to do what. [*Sitting next to* VANILLA] Now mistress, let's have a chat about this. This religion—it does seem to attract a lot of animosity.

VANILLA: Sticks and stones may break my bones but words will never hurt me.

LUDICRUS: Yes, well, it was more the 'sticks and stones' bit and the 'break my bones' bit that I was thinking about. You see, in Rome . . . well, you know lions?

VANILLA: Yes.

LUDICRUS: They throw you to them.

VANILLA: I don't mind. I like ice cream.

LUDICRUS: No, lions the animals.

VANILLA: Oh.

LUDICRUS: So you see, if you persist in this 'phase', there's a real chance you could end up as a takeaway.

VANILLA: I don't care! Let them do their worst! Let them beat me up and break my fingers one by one. Let them pull my teeth out and stick red hot needles into me! Let them . . . ooh . . . I think I need a glass of water. [*She exits SR.*]

LUDICRUS: [*To* CHICKEN] I'm not entirely convinced she understands. [*To* VANILLA] Anyway Mistress, I've got to keep an eye on you—you weren't planning on going anywhere? Mistress? Mistress? Oh no, where's she gone?

[LUDICRUS *rushes out SR, carrying the* CHICKEN. *Someone comes on and rearranges the chairs in a line SL.*]

VOICE: [*Offstage*] Come on ladies and gents! Genuine hand made togas—half price!

VOICE 2: [*Offstage*] Roast boar! Get your roast boar!

VOICE 3: [*Offstage*] Swords, lovely sharp swords, really sharp . . . oww!

[LUDICRUS *enters SL, still holding* CHICKEN. *He looks around him.*]

LUDICRUS: [*To audience*] This is the market place in Duodenum. A dirty, dusty place full of idiots, liars and thieves. Just like home really.

[*Enter* MYOPIA *SR. She sits on the floor DSC.*]

LUDICRUS: [*To audience*] Oh look—it's Myopia. Poor old dear. She's a beggar. Blind, you know. Can't see a thing.

[*While* LUDICRUS *is telling the audience this,* MYOPIA *gets out a newspaper and starts to read.*]

LUDICRUS: Absolutely and completely blind . . . wait a minute . . . [*To* MYOPIA] you can see!

MYOPIA: Yes isn't it wonderful! Don't I recognise your voice?

LUDICRUS: It's me—Ludicrus!

MYOPIA: Ludicrus—I remember you. You used to put buttons in my bowl because you thought I couldn't tell the difference.

LUDICRUS: Yes and you tried to train your guide dog to bite me.

MYOPIA: You're much uglier than I imagined you.

LUDICRUS: How dare you! Anyway, how come you can see?

MYOPIA: I'm cured! It's a miracle. It was them Christians, you see. I heard these people passing and I shouted out to them 'Alms for the poor' and they said, 'You've got some arms, have some eyes instead.' Then they prayed for me and I could see!

LUDICRUS: What a miracle! What a wonderful gift sight is!

MYOPIA: Yes, well, depends who you're looking at really.

LUDICRUS: Look—these Christians—one of them wasn't a girl?

MYOPIA: That's right. One of them wasn't a girl.

LUDICRUS: No, I mean was there a girl with them?

MYOPIA: Slim?

LUDICRUS: Yes.

MYOPIA: Young?

LUDICRUS: Yes.

MYOPIA: Called Vanilla?

LUDICRUS: Yes!

MYOPIA: Never heard of her. No, I'm only joking—she cured the beggar two along from me. The one with leprosy.

LUDICRUS: Leprosy! How could she heal someone with leprosy? She can't even spell it.

MYOPIA: Well, they're all like that. Just ordinary.

LUDICRUS: Where did she go?

MYOPIA: Prison.

LUDICRUS: Oh, that's all right . . . prison?

MYOPIA: Yes.

LUDICRUS: What for?

MYOPIA: For being different I suppose.

LUDICRUS: [*Panicking*] But this is awful! I'm supposed to keep her out of trouble! I'd better go.

MYOPIA: Er . . . before you go . . .
[*She shakes her begging bowl hopefully.*]

LUDICRUS: What are you doing? You don't need to beg now—you can see!

MYOPIA: I'm a professional beggar. You don't think I'm going to let a little handicap like perfect sight stop me from earning a living, do you?
[*Exit* MYOPIA *SR.* LUDICRUS *crosses SL.*]

LUDICRUS: [*To audience*] The prison! What a horrible place! You should see the cells—it would make you feel ill. They've got this hideous Mickey Mouse wallpaper up with a lilac carpet! Now then, how do I get in?

[*Enter* MAXIMUS *and a VIP SR.*]

MAXIMUS: And here we come to the fine prison building . . .

LUDICRUS: [*To audience*] The master! Oh no! He's due to tour the prison with his VIP!

[*He stands, trying to look invisible, a feat made more difficult by the fact that he is holding the* CHICKEN.]

MAXIMUS: [*Crossing towards SL*] Note the richly decorated portico and standing in the corner a hideous gargoyle . . . which reminds me of someone . . . Ludicrus! What are you doing here?

LUDICRUS: Master—don't go in there—you won't like it.

MAXIMUS: Don't be ridiculous. I've got to show this VIP round.

LUDICRUS: No, no, no, no, it's the gods you see—the gods! They came to me in a dream and warned me that if you went in there you wouldn't like it. You'd have a really bad time, and all your skin would turn yellow and your tail would fall off!

MAXIMUS: Don't be ridiculous. [*To VIP*] I do apologise for this delay.

LUDICRUS: Master please, take him somewhere else. Somewhere worse than the prison. How about the works canteen?

MAXIMUS: We are going in.

[*Sound effect: a loud prolonged explosion.* MAXIMUS *and* LUDICRUS *'fall' from side to side of the stage. The* CHICKEN *flies through the air. Then the sound fades and gradually they recover.*]

MAXIMUS: Pardon me.

LUDICRUS: An earthquake! [*To audience*] No it was, really. [*To* MAXIMUS] You see, master? I told you something would happen!

MAXIMUS: [*Dusting down the VIP*] Everything all right sir? I do apologise for the earthquake. Most unusual for the area I do assure you. Still, we should have been warned. I'll have the weathermen killed.

[VANILLA *enters, clambering through the 'wall' of chairs.*]

MAXIMUS: Now, as you can see the prison remains intact apart from that large crack which has just appeared and out of which my daughter is escaping. . . . Vanilla! What are you doing in jail?

VANILLA: Isn't it wonderful! It's a miracle!

MAXIMUS: [*Huge false laugh*] Ha-ha! She's a prison visitor you see, comes to help out, not one of these Jesusians, oh heavens no . . . I'm sure there's some perfectly reasonable explanation for all this . . . now moving right along, we see several more prisoners escaping and please note the gaoler lying unconscious in a corner where a large piece of masonry has fallen on him. [*To* VANILLA] Wait till I get you home!

[*He guides his VIP off SL.*]

VANILLA: Oh, he'll never understand!

LUDICRUS: Well, it's hard for him, suddenly finding his daughter changed. It's hard for us all. Coping with the healing and all that . . .

VANILLA: Oh, you heard about that . . .

LUDICRUS: Did you really heal someone from leprosy, mistress?

VANILLA: Not me—God. And then look what happened. They locked me up.

LUDICRUS: Well, you've got to expect opposition, mistress, you're different. And if you didn't encounter opposition, well, maybe that would mean you weren't worth bothering about. After all, it could be worse, it could be the lions! Come on, let's go home eh?

VANILLA: No. I've got to go to another meeting!

[*She rushes off SR.*]

LUDICRUS: But mistress, wait! I've got this chicken! Oh what's the use? See you tomorrow!

[LUDICRUS and CHICKEN *exit*.]

EPISODE THREE

Extra Characters:	VERANDA GIANTORTUS—A Christian woman.
	DAVID BEN NEVIS—Bishop of Duodenum
	VOICE—Offstage, in market place.
Plot:	VANILLA goes to the local fellowship who are weak and have compromised their faith. She decides to continue preaching herself.
Main Point:	The gospel is simple and we have a responsibility to keep preaching it.
Staging:	Chairs CS representing Roman couch.
Props/Costumes:	'1CC' magazine ('21CC' with the '2' tipp-exed out). Hammer and chisel, small stone slab. Box for VANILLA to stand on. Sunglasses for POMPUS. Eggs, lots of them.

JINGLE: 'Friends, Romans, Countrymen, lend us your ears . . .'

ANNOUNCER: Hi! We welcome you this morning with the latest chart news. Here's the new top three: at number three and a new entry, it's the Emperor Nero with 'I'm on Fire'. At number two there's the bright new talent, Cliff Richard, with 'Bachelor Boy'—he'll be around for a long time, take my word for it. And at number one it's Kylus Minogus with her follow up to 'I should be so lucky'; 'I should be smothered in raspberry jam and thrown to the lions actually'. And the weather today will be dry and dusty!

[*Enter* LUDICRUS *and* VANILLA *SL.* LUDICRUS *is still carrying the* CHICKEN.]

LUDICRUS: [*To audience*] Now, where am I? you might ask. Go on then. I'm glad you asked. I am at a meeting of Christians. And I'm here because I'm supposed to be looking after Vanilla. Her father, Maximus Gastroenteritis has told me to keep her out of trouble. So far she's sold her possessions, healed someone of leprosy, been arrested and thrown into jail and escaped during an earthquake. No trouble at all. And now we find ourselves here. [*To* VANILLA] Where are we?

VANILLA: Someone's house.

[*She sits on the couch and idly flicks through '1CC' magazine.*]

LUDICRUS: Very nice. Oughtn't we to be getting home? I feel stupid wandering around holding this chicken.

VANILLA: This is the local branch of the believers. There's the main meeting in Jerusalem and here in Duodenum they've set up a local fellowship.

[*Enter* VERANDA *SR.*]

VERANDA: Ah, you must be the new convert, the Roman. We've been warned about . . . er . . . expecting you. Would you care to carve in one of our forms? Just carve your name and address—for our records.

[*She hands* VANILLA *a stone tablet, a hammer and a chisel.* VANILLA *starts engraving.* LUDICRUS *sits on the couch.*]

VERANDA: [*Disdainfully*] Is this slave with you?

VANILLA: He's sort of a bodyguard.

VERANDA: How quaint. Now—my name's Veranda—Veranda Giantortue. You look tired, dear. Can I get you a cup of boiling water and dried leaves?

VANILLA: No, thank you, I've just come out of prison.

VERANDA: Prison? Oh, you've been visiting the poor dear prisoners have you?

VANILLA: No, we were arrested.

VERANDA: Arrested? Oh dear.

VANILLA: By soldiers.

VERANDA: Oh dear, oh dear.

VANILLA: But then God rescued us through a miraculous earthquake.

VERANDA: Oh dear, oh dear, oh dear.

VANILLA: Aren't you pleased for us?

VERANDA: Yes, delighted dear, except that . . . well, don't you think that you should go back and serve the rest of your sentence? There's no point *antagonising* people is there?

VANILLA: But I didn't do anything wrong. Just healed a few people that's all.

VERANDA: Oh you're a physician. And so young.

VANILLA: No, we healed them through prayer.

VERANDA: Oh yes—prayer. Well we don't really go in for that sort of thing here. No, we're simple souls here.

VANILLA: I just preached the good news.

VERANDA: They're chocolates aren't they?

VANILLA: No—about Jesus.

VERANDA: No, no, no, don't tell me—the name's very familiar . . .

VANILLA: Surely you know who I'm talking about?

VERANDA: Well, has he filled in one of our cards?

VANILLA: Jesus. The Christ.

VERANDA: No, I don't think he's ever been here.

VANILLA: I don't believe this.

VERANDA: Oh—you mean Our Lord and Saviour Most High, Rod of Jesse, the new Melchizedek.

VANILLA: Do I?

VERANDA: Oh—here comes David—I'm sure he'll be able to explain some of these deeper theological ideas.

[*Enter* DAVID BEN NEVIS *SR.* VANILLA *and* LUDICRUS *rise.*]

VERANDA: This is David Ben Nevis. A Jew.

LUDICRUS: Bless you. Oh sorry, I thought you sneezed.

DAVID: Hello, pleased to meet you.

[*He gives* VANILLA *an extremely limp handshake.*]

VERANDA: Now this young lady has been preaching the gospel.

DAVID: Oh dear . . . now what exactly were you saying then?

VANILLA: Just about Jesus dying and rising from the dead.

DAVID: Well of course, it all depends what you mean by 'rising' and 'dying' and 'from' and 'the'. Because we have to accept that in modern philosophy there is always more than one way to look at any given question. We must beware that we don't fall into the trap of believing there is an objective, oetiological truism, but rather that there are a series of perceived images or metaphors, and that we should, for want of a better word, 'preach' an holistic, syncretistic gospel.

[*He exits SR.*]

VANILLA: Who was that?

VERANDA: That was the bishop. Now, can I put you down for the flower rota?

VANILLA: But what about preaching the gospel?

VERANDA: We *do* preach the gospel. Just the one *we* want to preach, that's all.

[LUDICRUS *starts to leave SL.*]

VANILLA: Where are you going? I thought you were supposed to guard me?

LUDICRUS: I don't think you'll get into any trouble here. These people are more Roman than the Romans. Me and the chicken are going home.

[*Exit* VERANDA *and* VANILLA *SR.* LUDICRUS *moves SL. Fanfare. Enter* POMPUS *SR.*]

LUDICRUS: How do you do that?

POMPUS: Centurion Pompus Hippopotamus of the Jerusalem Garrison is here!

LUDICRUS: Wotcha.

POMPUS: My esteemed brother-in-law Maximus Gastroenteritis says, 'How's it going with Vanilla?'

LUDICRUS: Oh fine, fine, no trouble. She's at church.

POMPUS: Church? Which one? I must go and break it up.

LUDICRUS: The local one—here in Duodenum.

POMPUS: Oh that one. We don't bother persecuting that one. It persecutes itself.

LUDICRUS: Yeah, a more ineffective bunch I've yet to see . . .

[POMPUS *is standing facing* LUDICRUS *with his back to SR.* VANILLA *enters SR and puts a soapbox down on the stage.*]

LUDICRUS: [*Seeing* VANILLA *over* POMPUS'*s shoulder*] She won't . . . get . . . into trouble . . . there . . . [*He slows as he sees* VANILLA *about to preach.*]

POMPUS: Are you all right? You've gone pale.

LUDICRUS: Oughtn't you to be going?

POMPUS: What?

LUDICRUS: Well, I mean—haven't you got legionaries to parade, or a massacre to commit or something?

POMPUS: No, it's a quiet day today, nothing to worry about.

VANILLA: [*Preaching to offstage*] Friends, Romans, Countrymen, lend me your ears. I want to talk to you about Jesus. Now you all know me—Vanilla, daughter of Maximus Gastroenteritis. Oh—and there's my Uncle, Centurion Pompus Hippopotamus!

[POMPUS *puts on dark glasses and attempts to look inconspicuous.*]

VANILLA: Now the good news is that Jesus died for you . . .

POMPUS: Perfectly safe, eh? Nothing to worry about, eh? She's making a spectacle of herself. I'm going to have to arrest her you know.

LUDICRUS: No, no, wait a minute, don't get psychological yet. Let me handle this. I think we can use the mob against her, you know, stir up the people. They'll pelt her with eggs and rubbish and all that and that'll shut her up.

POMPUS: Good idea. That'll make her think twice about speaking out in public.

[LUDICRUS *rushes offstage SL.*]

VANILLA: So you see, we all need forgiveness. It's so simple.

LUDICRUS: [*Shouting from offstage*] Oh yeah? Sez you! I

mean how do we know you're not lying? How do we know you're not a subversive pinko spy? Come on everybody, let's get the Christian. Let's chuck these eggs at her! Er . . . everybody?

VANILLA: No wait, please . . . he didn't mean it . . .

[*Enter* LUDICRUS *SL. He is covered in eggs.*]

VOICE: [*From offstage*] And don't interrupt again.

LUDICRUS: Thank you very much. So much for my powers of rabble-rousing. I think you'll have to arrest her.

POMPUS: Are you kidding? I've just got this uniform back from the cleaners. No, this is the time for tactical retreat.

[LUDICRUS *moves SR. Exit* VANILLA *and* POMPUS *SR. Enter* GORILLA *SL. She reclines on the couch.*]

GORILLA: Hello Ludicrus. Eggs? Are they good for the complexion?

LUDICRUS: Not very.

GORILLA: Why are you wearing them then?

LUDICRUS: I stirred up the mob against myself.

GORILLA: Where's Vanilla? You were supposed to be keeping an eye on her.

LUDICRUS: She's in the market place.

GORILLA: Shopping?

LUDICRUS: Preaching.

GORILLA: Preaching! Oh no! How could you let this happen?

LUDICRUS: [*Angry*] I disclaim responsibility! Your daughter is beyond control—and that's your fault because you brought her up. I can't control what she says and does, or what happens to her. In the past few hours I have been threatened with death, accused of burglary, hit by an earthquake and pelted by a mob and I've had to do all this while wandering around town holding an oven ready chicken! Well, I resign!

GORILLA: [*Pause*] You can't. You're a slave. Now get yourself cleaned up and go and find out what's happened to our daughter.

[*Exit* GORILLA *SL.*]

LUDICRUS: [*To audience*] Oh yes, very funny. You see what it's like being a slave? I can't understand what makes her do it, really I can't. She never used to get up and preach before. It's as if she's broken loose or something. Free. I wish I could be freed. Now that really would be good news . . . oh well . . . it could be worse. I could be an actor. See you tomorrow.

[LUDICRUS *exits.*]

EPISODE FOUR

Extra Characters:	FLATIAH—Member of obscure Jewish sect.
	GASFIAH—Member of obscure Jewish sect.
	COMMENTATOR—On Radio Judea.
Plot:	VANILLA has disappeared. LUDICRUS meets two members of a Jewish sect. VANILLA turns up at the gladiator fights and tries to disrupt them.
Main Point:	As Christians, we are supposed to take action, not hide in a mass of doctrines, rules and regulations.
Props/Costumes:	Shopping bag containing toga for GORILLA. GASFIAH and FLATIAH are dressed in black and wear big black beards.

JINGLE: 'Friends, Romans, Countrymen, lend us your ears . . .'

ANNOUNCER: Hi! We welcome you this morning with the latest sports news from the Coliseum. Roman Legionaries 3—Barbarians 0; Pretorian Guard 1—Milwall Supporters 3. Lions 74—Christians 0. And the result of the 3.30 chariot race from Kempton

Park was first Ben Hur, 6–4 favourite, and all the others died in horrific crashes. Weather? You've guessed it—dry and dusty.

[*Enter* LUDICRUS, *holding* CHICKEN.]

LUDICRUS: [*To audience*] Well, as you can see, I have been de-egged after my unfortunate encounter with the mob in the Duodenum market place. And here I am, combing the town for Vanilla—daughter of Maximus Gastroenteritis etc., etc. And can I find her? No—I cannot.

[*Fanfare. Enter* POMPUS *SR*.]

POMPUS: Hail!

LUDICRUS: It's the weatherman.

POMPUS: Centurion Pompus Hippopotamus is here!

LUDICRUS: Grovel, grovel, grovel, grovel, grovel.

POMPUS: All right, all right. Where is it? Where's this riot?

LUDICRUS: It's over, you great pudding. They've all gone home.

POMPUS: Oh, that's a relief. Thought for a moment I'd have to arrest little Vanilla. I've always had a soft spot for her.

LUDICRUS: A peat-bog springs to mind.

POMPUS: Oh well, there's still plenty to do. Are you going to the games this afternoon?

LUDICRUS: What games?

POMPUS: What games? The games in the circus of course. Games of life and death, of men fighting against incredible odds—chariot racing, gladiator combat, tiddlywinks. Should be a great fight this afternoon—Brunus against Tysus.

LUDICRUS: What's Brunus using?

POMPUS: Sword and shield.

LUDICRUS: And Tysus?

POMPUS: Ferret.

LUDICRUS: Ferret?

POMPUS: Sticks it straight down his opponent's armour. While his opponent is trying to remove it he clubs him to death using his other weapon.

LUDICRUS: Oh, he's got another weapon then?

POMPUS: Of course! You don't think he'd go out and fight a man armed with just a ferret do you? That'd be suicide.

LUDICRUS: Well, I thought it sounded a bit strange.

POMPUS: No, no, no—he's got a badger as well.

LUDICRUS: A badger.

POMPUS: Exactly.

LUDICRUS: Let me get this right—Tysus rushes out, sticks a ferret down his opponent's armour and then clubs him to death . . . with . . . a . . . badger.

POMPUS: He's unique. Some of the best psychology you've ever seen.

LUDICRUS: Well, I'm not going. I don't like gladiator fights. They're barbaric.

POMPUS: Nonsense. A knife in the guts never hurt anyone. It's what the public wants.

LUDICRUS: What about this new game—very popular in the provinces? Two teams of eleven men kick an inflated bladder and try and score goals.

POMPUS: Is that all?

LUDICRUS: More or less.

POMPUS: Doesn't anyone get killed?

LUDICRUS: Depends who you're playing really. If it's Wimbledon . . .

POMPUS: Anyway, I must go. Farewell, slave.

[*Exit* POMPUS *SL*.]

LUDICRUS: [*To audience*] I ask you! Two grown men fighting to the death to provide entertainment for the masses. It's disgusting! I wonder what time it starts?

[*Enter* GORILLA *SR, carrying shopping bag*.]

GORILLA: Ludicrus! Have you found Vanilla yet?

LUDICRUS: I'm afraid not, mistress.

GORILLA: I'm distraught with worry. I'm so worried that I had to go out and buy a new toga.

[*She shows* LUDICRUS *her purchase*.]

LUDICRUS: Very nice—where did you get it?

GORILLA: Posterus.

LUDICRUS: Posterus?

GORILLA: Latin for next. Anyway—you still haven't found her?

LUDICRUS: I'm sorry mistress, she's disappeared. Your brother Centurion Pompus came to arrest her, but she'd gone. He went off to keep order at the games.

GORILLA: What games?

LUDICRUS: Gladiators. Brunus and his sword against Tysus, a ferret and a badger.

GORILLA: [*Disgusted*] Gladiators! How disgusting! [*Pause*] What time does it start?

LUDICRUS: I don't know.

GORILLA: Well I'll go and take a little look. Perhaps it will take my mind off the nastier side of life.

LUDICRUS: Oh yes, I always find watching a man being clubbed to death with a badger so relaxing . . .

GORILLA: Just before I go, why are you holding that chicken?

LUDICRUS: Because if I let go it falls on the ground and gets dirty.

GORILLA: [*Apparently satisfied with this answer*] Oh, of course.

[*Exit* GORILLA *SL. Enter* GASFIAH *and* FLATIAH *SR.*]

LUDICRUS: [*To audience*] Oh look who's coming! The Jews have this strict religion you see—all laws—do this, do that. You see these kind of people all over the place.

FLATIAH: [*Seeing* LUDICRUS] Aaaahhh!! Infidel!

GASFIAH: Aaaah!

LUDICRUS: What?

FLATIAH: Look at him! Look!

LUDICRUS: Who? Me?

GASFIAH: Breaking the law!

FLATIAH: The sacred law!

LUDICRUS: How?

GASFIAH: Holding a chicken!

FLATIAH: In the right hand!

GASFIAH: In public!

FLATIAH: On a Thursday morning!

GASFIAH: Unclean! Unclean!

FLATIAH: The law has been transgressed!

GASFIAH: The sacred law that is sacred and that shouldn't be transgressed!

FLATIAH: The law that is called sacred and that shouldn't be transgressed because it's sacred and you shouldn't transgress sacred laws . . .

GASFIAH: The sacred law . . .

LUDICRUS: Yes all right, all right, you've made your point. What exactly have I done wrong?

FLATIAH: It is against the law for a Jew to be seen in public holding a chicken.

LUDICRUS: But I'm not Jewish.

FLATIAH: [*Pause*] Oh—that's all right then.
GASFIAH: What are you then?
LUDICRUS: A slave. I work for Maximus Gastroenteritis.
GASFIAH: Maximus?
FLATIAH: Gastroenteritis?
GASFIAH: Has he a daughter?
FLATIAH: Called Vanilla?
LUDICRUS: Yes.
GASFIAH: Aaaahhh!
FLATIAH: Unclean! Unclean!
GASFIAH: Slave in the household of a Christian infidel!
FLATIAH: Holding a chicken!
GASFIAH: In the right hand!
LUDICRUS: Look, will you shut up! Who are you?
GASFIAH: I am Gasfiah.
FLATIAH: I am Flatiah.
LUDICRUS: What are you—Sadducees or Pharisees?
FLATIAH: Neither. We're Celeries.
LUDICRUS: Celeries?
GASFIAH: We believe in everything that the others believe in . . .
FLATIAH: But we also believe bananas are sinful.
LUDICRUS: You're not Christians then?
GASFIAH: Aaaahhh!
FLATIAH: Infidel!
GASFIAH: He spoke the word.
FLATIAH: Whilst holding a chicken!
LUDICRUS: Look, look, calm down. I'm just a slave. What do I know? There's no need to go bananas.
GASFIAH: Aaaah! Sinful!
FLATIAH: Infidel!
LUDICRUS: So what do you do, apart from yell?
FLATIAH: Do?

GASFIAH: The law is not about 'doing' things, infidel. It's about *not* doing things.

FLATIAH: Like holding chickens.

LUDICRUS Yes, well, if you'll excuse me. I have to go and see the gladiators fight.

FLATIAH: Gladiators?

GASFIAH: Fighting?

FLATIAH: Against the law!

GASFIAH: Unclean!

FLATIAH: Unclean!

GASFIAH: Unclean! ... what time does it start then?

LUDICRUS: Any minute now. Oh, before you go ...

GASFIAH: Yes?

LUDICRUS: Christians.

[*Exit* GASFIAH and FLATIAH *SR, wailing. Exit* LUDICRUS *SL.*]

COMMENTATOR: [*Voice from offstage*] You join us in the first round of this heavyweight fight—Brunus versus Tysus. And Brunus tries a few thrusts with his sword, trying to hit Tysus in the ferret, Tysus standing there, waving his badger menacingly ... wait a minute ... there appears to be a disturbance in the crowd, a girl has leapt down and appears to be trying to get in between the gladiators ... she's shouting out ... the crowd are invading, there's some people trying to stop her—a slave, a centurion, oh dear there's chaos here now. The slave has got a ferret up the nose and the centurion has been felled by the badger ... the crowd are swarming on ... it's terrible, it's a pitch invasion ...!

[*Enter* LUDICRUS *SL, staggering, supporting* GORILLA.]

GORILLA: The shame! The shame!

LUDICRUS: Never mind the shame—I got a ferret stuffed up my nose.

GORILLA: Why? Why did Vanilla try to stop the gladiators? They weren't harming anyone.

LUDICRUS: Didn't you hear her? She said God wanted it stopped . . .

GORILLA: Where did she go?

LUDICRUS: I don't know, she disappeared in the chaos.

GORILLA: What's happened to her? She never used to be like this. She would never have had the nerve!

LUDICRUS: She's changed, mistress. There's something inside her, it makes her do these things.

[*Enter* FLATIAH *and* GASFIAH *SL.*]

FLATIAH: Aaahhhh! There he is!

GASFIAH: Slave in the house of the infidel!

FLATIAH: Still holding a chicken!

GASFIAH: Have you no shame?

GORILLA: [*To* LUDICRUS] Who are these people?

LUDICRUS: Banana haters. [*To* FLATIAH *and* GASFIAH] What are you on about?

FLATIAH: Pitch invader!

GASFIAH: Hooligan!

FLATIAH: Slave in the house of a yobbo!

LUDICRUS: Oh you were there then? I thought you didn't agree with all the violence?

FLATIAH: We went to make sure it was unlawful.

GASFIAH: And anyway—we had money on Brunus to win.

LUDICRUS: So much for your high morals.

FLATIAH: We are within the law.

GASFIAH: We are pure.

FLATIAH: We have done nothing wrong!

LUDICRUS: No you've done nothing at all, have you? You 'disapprove' of it but you don't do anything to stop it. Well, at least Vanilla did something. At least her religion isn't just about feeling holier than everyone else. At least she isn't a fraud.

FLATIAH: Infidel!

GASFIAH: Chicken-holder!

FLATIAH: Transgressor of the sacred law which is sacred and which should never. . . .

LUDICRUS: Oh—'Christians!'

FLATIAH: Aaaaaaahhhhhh!

GASFIAH: Aaahhhhhhhhhh!

[They rush off SL, covering their ears.]

GORILLA: Ludicrus, you seem to attract the strangest people.

LUDICRUS: Yeah, I'm surrounded by loonies. Oh, present company excluded, mistress. Come on, you go home, you've had a nasty shock.

[Exit GORILLA *SR.]*

LUDICRUS: *[To audience]* So there we are. Another day, another ferret up the nose. I dunno, mistress Vanilla acted in a totally unreasonable, outrageous way and you know something? I'm proud of her. Because she does things. She don't just pay lip service. She takes risks, and whatever you think about what she believes, at least she stands up for it. She's a real Christian.

FLATIAH:
GASFIAH: [*Offstage*] Aaaahhhhhh! Infidel! [*Etc.*]
LUDICRUS: [*To audience*] See you around.
[*Exit* LUDICRUS *and* CHICKEN.]

EPISODE FIVE

Extra Characters: LOOFAH—The soothsayer.

Plot: VANILLA's disappearance prompts her parents to call in the soothsayer to tell them what has happened.

Main Point: That the occult, however innocent it seems, is dangerous and causes harm.

Props/Costumes: LUDICRUS has a broom. MAXIMUS has a scroll (his horoscope) and some money to give to LOOFAH. The RUBBER CHICKEN has been stuffed with suitably unexpected things to produce from its innards. LOOFAH wears a ragged, dirty robe and a big cloak. She is generally wild-eyed and unkempt.

Remarks: I think it's worth pointing out that this sketch *condemns* horoscopes and suchlike. There have been a few odd-balls who assume that if you portray something, and worse, if you *joke* about it, then you must approve of it. Which means, if we take Shakespeare as an example, that he approved of rape, torture, killing, cutting people's tongues out, and serving people a pie filled with their close relatives. You have to portray something to condemn it. The whole point of this sketch is that no matter how innocuous or even inaccurate the 'prophecy' it is still damaging and dangerous.

JINGLE: 'Friends, Romans, Countrymen, lend us your ears . . .'

ANNOUNCER: Radio Judea here saying a great Gooooood Morning to you all on another dry and dusty day. If it's your birthday today, happy birthday and here's your horoscope. Your lucky number is 'VIII', your lucky animal is 'gerbil' and your lucky stone is 'gall'. You will have an uneventful day today but some time in the afternoon a pig may fall on your head. So take care out there and wear a hat. That horoscope comes to you from the Delphic Oracle in Greece, so if you want to know any more—just page the oracle!

[*Enter* LUDICRUS. *He stands SC behind couch.*]

LUDICRUS: Well now, the story so far. Vanilla, whose exploits include healing the sick, selling all her possessions, causing an earthquake and disrupting the games, seems to have disappeared. It's very mysterious and most worrying, especially as I was supposed to keep her from harm and if she's in trouble then I know a certain centurion who will happily use some psychology on me. As you can imagine, the family are worried sick.

[*Enter* GORILLA *SL, singing happily. She reclines on the couch.*]

GORILLA: Oh, Ludicrus, there you are. No sign I suppose?

LUDICRUS: I'm afraid not, mistress. I have searched every nook and cranny. Some of them quite unpleasant nooks and crannies, I can tell you.

GORILLA: Ah well, can't be helped. [*Resumes singing*]

LUDICRUS: You're taking all this very well.

GORILLA: Well, you'll be glad to know that it'll all be sorted out soon. I've hired the soothsayer, Loofah.

LUDICRUS: Not her! Not that old crow!

GORILLA: What do you mean? She has powerful spells.

LUDICRUS: Powerful smells, more like. I'd better get a new supply of air-freshener in.

GORILLA: She is touched by the gods.

LUDICRUS: Well, she's certainly touched. She's several legionaries short of a cohort.

[*Enter* MAXIMUS *SL, holding scroll.*]

MAXIMUS: Ah Ludicrus, this is a sorry business. I just know my daughter is in trouble. It's this sect she's involved in, this hocus-pocus, this mumbo-jumbo, this . . .

GORILLA: Jiggery-pokery.

MAXIMUS: I know. Anyway, I have decided to consult the gods. I have been looking up my future.

LUDICRUS: A clever trick if you can do it.

MAXIMUS: My horoscope.

LUDICRUS: Oh master—you don't believe all that?

MAXIMUS: This horoscope was drawn up by one of the leading astrologers—Russelus Granti. It's true.

LUDICRUS: How do you know?

MAXIMUS: It cost me a lot of money, it must be true.

GORILLA: What does it say for today, oh husband?

MAXIMUS: [*Reading from scroll*] Venus is in conjunction with Mars. Saturn has passed through Aquarius. Meanwhile, the small blobby star next to Orion has moved.

GORILLA: Oh woe is us!

LUDICRUS: Is that bad then?

GORILLA: Of course. Especially the small blobby star.

MAXIMUS: It says, 'Be careful today—something may happen to you.'

LUDICRUS: Remarkable. 'Something may happen to you.' Well of course something may happen to you! Something happens to you every day.

GORILLA: What does it say about me?

LUDICRUS: It says, 'You are very beautiful and talented and your husband should give you lots of money to spend on clothes' . . . wait a minute, this looks like *your* writing.

GORILLA: It's a miracle! Not only do his predictions come true, but he actually writes in the handwriting of the people he predicts about!

MAXIMUS: *You* wrote this.

GORILLA: It was worth a try.

LUDICRUS: Useless! You see, master, he hasn't got a thing right.

MAXIMUS: Well, let's see what he says about you.

LUDICRUS: Yeah, no-one could possibly predict what's happened to me this week.

MAXIMUS: [*Reading*] 'This week you will be accused of theft, threatened with beheading, caught in an earthquake, pelted with eggs, and hit with a ferret.'

LUDICRUS: [*Pause*] Huh! It was a lucky guess.

MAXIMUS: 'Also you will meet a tall dark idiot.'

LUDICRUS: Yes, well, I think those things are wrong. And anyway, I haven't met the idiot, yet.

[*Enter* LOOFAH *SR.*]

LOOFAH: Woe! Woe!

LUDICRUS: Oh—tell a lie.

LOOFAH: Woe to this city, for it will be afflicted! It will have plagues and pestilence and other things beginning with a 'p'! It will face the wrath of the gods and it will turn into a herring!

LUDICRUS: A herring?

LOOFAH: A herring with roller-skates on.

LUDICRUS: I think you've been drinking the metal polish.

LOOFAH: So say the gods.

MAXIMUS: Oh Loofah, oh soothsayer, say us the sooth!

GORILLA: Yes, we seek the truth oh mouthpiece of the gods.

MAXIMUS: Sooth us the truth and the proof.

GORILLA: Our rude young daughter has disappeared!

MAXIMUS: Oh Loofah, sooth us the truth and the proof of our uncouth youth from your mooth . . . mouth.

LOOFAH: I will read the entrails.

LUDICRUS: The entrails?

LOOFAH: The innards . . . of a chicken.

LUDICRUS: [*Producing the* CHICKEN *from behind the couch.*] Oh well—here's one I prepared earlier.

[*He throws it across to* LOOFAH.]

LOOFAH: [*Taking* CHICKEN.] The innards of this animal will tell us what the future holds. Let us remove them.

[*Various objects are produced from within the* CHICKEN*—a string of hankies tied together, sausages etc.*]

LUDICRUS: That's a heck of a chicken.

GORILLA: What do these entrails tell us, oh Loofah?

MAXIMUS: Yes, sooth us the truth and the . . .

LUDICRUS: Don't start all that again.

LOOFAH: [*Dramatically*] They say your daughter is dead!

MAXIMUS: Dead?

LOOFAH: You will have no more to do with her.

LUDICRUS: What are you talking about?

LOOFAH: The entrails do not lie.

LUDICRUS: Yes well, the entrails may not lie, but as for others . . .

GORILLA: Dead!

LUDICRUS: Don't listen to her, mistress. She doesn't know what she's talking about! She can't read her own name, let alone a chicken.

MAXIMUS: Dead!

GORILLA: Woe!

MAXIMUS: Dead!

LOOFAH: That will be three silver pieces.

MAXIMUS: [*Calmly*] Oh, right. [*Hands over the money, then dramatically*] Dead!

LOOFAH: I can do no more.

LUDICRUS: No—you've done enough.

LOOFAH: [*To* LUDICRUS] Disbeliever, I curse thee! Let thy hair turn puce and thy nose turn into a turtle, thy body will shrivel with sickness and thy toes . . .

LUDICRUS: Oh shut up.

[LOOFAH *exits SR, deflated.*]

GORILLA: Dead!

LUDICRUS: Look, let's just calm down a bit, shall we? We don't know this is true.

MAXIMUS: We do! The chicken is a message from the gods.

LUDICRUS: It's not from the gods, it's from Sainsbury's. The gods had nothing to do with it.

GORILLA: She's dead!

MAXIMUS: She's gone!

[*Enter* VANILLA *SR.*]

LUDICRUS: She's just come into the kitchen.

GORILLA: Aahhh! A ghost!

VANILLA: It's me!

MAXIMUS: Is it really you, daughter?

VANILLA: I think so.

GORILLA: Oh how wonderful! [*Suddenly angry*] Where have you been? We've been worried sick about you!

VANILLA: I've been at a prayer meeting.

GORILLA: Oh no! You're not still involved with these people, are you?

VANILLA: We were praying about the occult. We were praying that all the soothsayers would get it wrong.

LUDICRUS: Well that one certainly worked.

MAXIMUS: [*Furious*] How dare you! How dare you pray against the religion of the Roman Empire. You know I have forbidden you to meet with these people: You're too young to get mixed up in this hocus-pocus, this mumbo-jumbo, this . . .

GORILLA: Jiggery-pokery.

MAXIMUS: I know!!

VANILLA: But I'm not the mixed-up one—you are. Look at you all—attacking a poor little innocent chicken.

MAXIMUS: You have made your choice. You have thrown over the old faiths that your family has held since time immemorial. Well, now we cast you out.

VANILLA: What do you mean?

MAXIMUS: Loofah said you were dead, and dead you shall be. You are dead to me as long as you persist in this . . . this . . .

GORILLA: Jiggery-pokery.

MAXIMUS: Shut up! [*Regaining composure*] As long as you remain with this sect it will be to me as though you don't exist.

VANILLA: But Daddy . . .

MAXIMUS: [*To* GORILLA] And this is all your fault!
[*Exit* MAXIMUS *SL.*]

GORILLA: [*To* LUDICRUS] Now look what you've done!
[*Exit* GORILLA *SL, leaving* VANILLA *standing alone.*]

LUDICRUS: [*To audience*] You see what happens? Even if the prophecies aren't true they still damage. Evil, that's what they are. Evil. If you think they're harmless then look what they've done to this family, let alone this chicken. Oh well, I guess it will sort itself out. Anyway . . . I hope so . . . see you tomorrow.
[*Exit* LUDICRUS, *comforting* VANILLA.]

EPISODE SIX

Plot: MAXIMUS becomes the new chief of police. One of the conditions, however, is that he arrests his own daughter.

Main Point: Christianity is not an easy option. It means sacrifices and it puts us into conflict with others.

Props/Costumes: Ironing board, iron and pile of clothes for LUDICRUS. Letter for MAXIMUS. Catalogues for GORILLA. Letter for POMPUS.

JINGLE: 'Friends, Romans, Countrymen, lend us your ears . . .'

ANNOUNCER: Radio Judea here, and the big news of the day is that Pontius Pilate has been replaced. He will move on to be Governor of Outer Mongolia. No transfer fee has been announced. His successor will be Governor Cornelius Crismusbonus—a man renowned for his tough stands on defence, security and people's heads. Of the recent political unrest, Governor Crismusbonus has said, 'I don't mind people disagreeing with me, so long as they don't mind me splitting their nostrils with a boat hook.' The weather today will be thunderstorms, torrential rain, hail, snow and a plague of frogs.

[*Enter* LUDICRUS *SR. There is an ironing board set up, SR.* LUDICRUS *stands and irons a huge pile of ironing.*]

LUDICRUS: [*To audience*] A new governor has arrived, as you've just heard. Not a particularly pleasant type. Especially strong on suppressing all minority groups—you know, agitators, dissidents, humans, that sort of thing.

[*Enter* MAXIMUS *and* GORILLA *SL.* GORILLA *is looking, and feeling, very frail. She sits on the couch and leafs through some catalogues whilst* MAXIMUS *prepares for work.*]

MAXIMUS: [*Crossing to CS*] Do I look all right?

LUDICRUS: You look fine, master. Well, as fine as you're ever likely to look.

MAXIMUS: No hairs on my toga?

LUDICRUS: No.

MAXIMUS: Or dandruff?

LUDICRUS: No.

MAXIMUS: Or . . . [*whispers*]

LUDICRUS: [*Checks his sleeve*] No. And anyway you wouldn't have that trouble if you used a hankie like everyone else.

MAXIMUS: Big day today, Ludicrus. New boss arriving.

LUDICRUS: So I heard.

MAXIMUS: Could be promotion for me, if I play my cards right.

LUDICRUS: Hooray.

MAXIMUS: It's important. I don't want to spend my life as a minor official. I'd do anything to gain power, anything. I don't want to be at other people's beck and call. I want power! Power, do you hear! I want to be feared and respected and to order people about. I want to be in charge!

GORILLA: Oh, stop shouting.

MAXIMUS: [*Meekly*] Yes dear.

GORILLA: Oh, I feel exhausted.

MAXIMUS: Well, I'd better be off.

GORILLA: Yes dear. Have a nice day among the sewage.

MAXIMUS: Oh you can scoff. It may be sewage to you, but it's bread and butter to me.

GORILLA: Oh, I forgot, there was a letter for you—here.

MAXIMUS: It's from the governor, it could be important!

GORILLA: I'm sorry, it came among a load of slave catalogues. I got it mixed up.

MAXIMUS: [*Reading letter*] But this is great news! Promotion! Promotion, do you hear? I'm to be head of police, providing . . . providing . . . oh . . .

GORILLA: What is it dear?

MAXIMUS: Nothing. It's nothing. I'm to be new head of police. Governor Crismushonus has been very good to me. It's what I've always wanted—more power, more influence, more money. We just have to make certain 'adjustments' that's all.

GORILLA: What do you mean?

MAXIMUS: When you want something . . . if you want something badly enough, you have to take difficult decisions. Painful decisions.

LUDICRUS: Some kind of operation, is it, master?

MAXIMUS: Shut up.

GORILLA: Well, if it means more money, dear. You do what you have to do.

MAXIMUS: Right.

GORILLA: I can buy new togas. We can move!

MAXIMUS: Exactly. This letter—it's a once-in-a-lifetime chance. I must go and see Pompus.

[*Exit* MAXIMUS *SL.*]

LUDICRUS: Oh well, at least I didn't have to kiss him this morning.

GORILLA: [*Rising*] Imagine, Ludicrus. We're going to be rich!

LUDICRUS: Yes—what did he mean about painful decisions, I wonder?

GORILLA: Oh, it's nothing. He does tend to over-dramatise things.

LUDICRUS: Perhaps he's got to sack someone.

GORILLA: No, he wouldn't find that difficult. He's always enjoyed sacking people.

LUDICRUS: Oh well, I don't suppose it's important.

GORILLA: Well, whatever he has to do is all right by me. As long as there's more money at the end of the day! Oh I'm so happy! I can buy a new slave. They're having a sale down at BHS.

LUDICRUS: BHS?

GORILLA: British Home Slaves. 500 sestertii minimum when you trade in your old slave for a new model.

LUDICRUS: Oh and I'm just a clapped out old banger I suppose?

GORILLA: Latest model offers over six foot tall, thirteen stone, six litres capacity, choice of colour in hair and eyes.

LUDICRUS: Which make is that?

GORILLA: BMW—Big Male Worker. Corrrrrr! Talk about Vorsprung Durch Technic.

[*She exits SL.*]

LUDICRUS: [*To audience*] It's disgusting. People like me, bought and sold. Of course, I haven't always been a slave. No, I had to work my way up. I used to be one step lower than a slave. I used to be a teacher. Don't know why I bothered, really.

[*Fanfare.*]

LUDICRUS: Oh here we go. Colonel Blimp's arrived.

[*Enter* POMPUS *SR.*]

POMPUS: Slave! Centurion Pompus Hippopotamus is here!

LUDICRUS: [*Sarcastically*] Oh great magnificent one! Oh illustrious warrior! What joy it is to feast my unworthy eyes on a huge muscular lump like yourself.

POMPUS: [*Flattered*] Yeah, I am pretty muscular aren't I?

LUDICRUS: Of course you are. Especially between the ears. What is it you wish, oh spangle of the cosmos?

POMPUS: Ah, well, I'm here on official business.

LUDICRUS: Ah—it's not about the chariot, is it? You see I meant to get the licence but you know how it is . . . well . . . it's in the post, that's it, it's in the post . . . and I didn't mean to double park it, only the horse ran out of fuel . . .

POMPUS: No, it's not about the chariot.

LUDICRUS: Oh.

POMPUS: But all that was very interesting. It's this letter from Maximus. He's got promotion.

LUDICRUS: Yes, I know.

POMPUS: Providing I arrest Vanilla.

LUDICRUS: What? His own daughter? He sent you to arrest his own daughter? You can't do that!

POMPUS: Here—read it. [*Anxiously*] I . . . I'm not very good at this sort of thing. I'm better at psychology. You tell her, eh? There's a good chap. I'll be outside.

[*Exit* POMPUS *SR.* LUDICRUS *reads the letter and while he reads* VANILLA *enters behind, from SL. She carries a bag of clothes.*]

LUDICRUS: [*Reading*] 'From Maximus Gastroenteritis to esteemed brother-in-law Pompus Hippopotamus. The great and glorious Governor Crismusbonus has made me Controller of the police and my first job will be to clear out all the Christians. To this end, please nip along and arrest Vanilla. I know we have certain family ties, but, after all, the good of the empire must come first. I'm sure you understand . . .'

VANILLA: I thought this might happen. I'm all packed.

LUDICRUS: I can't believe he'd do this.

VANILLA: It's his job. He always wanted to be in charge of people.

LUDICRUS: Why don't you run away? I could sabotage the centurion's horse—stop him following you.

VANILLA: I'm quite prepared, Ludicrus.

LUDICRUS: All right then. Go on. Get arrested. See if I care.

[*He irons for a moment but is unable to keep silent.*]

LUDICRUS: [*Upset and angry*] I thought this was supposed to be a religion of peace? I thought it was all about harmony and stuff . . . ?

VANILLA: I can't help people's reactions, can I? It is a peaceful religion, but, well . . . it changes people, doesn't it? And sometimes that change is so great, you no longer fit in. You're upset.

LUDICRUS: No I'm not.

VANILLA: Then why are you ironing the chicken?

[He has inadvertently pulled the CHICKEN *from the pile of clothes and is giving it a quick once-over with the iron.]*

LUDICRUS: It got creased after all it's been through.

VANILLA: Well, I'd better go and face the music. It'll be all right. I've been in prison before, remember?

LUDICRUS: This time is different. I can feel it.

VANILLA: Well, I won't be alone. Jesus never said it would be easy. But he did say he'd always be there. You know—I always felt you understood. You never once said I was wrong. Maybe you ought to think about it for yourself.

LUDICRUS: Yes, well, I've got all this ironing to do, if you don't mind.

VANILLA: Goodbye, Ludicrus.

[She moves SR and has almost exited.]

LUDICRUS: Goodbye little one. Take care.

[Exit VANILLA *SR.]*

LUDICRUS: *[To audience]* Yeah? What are you lot staring at? It's not any easier for you, you know. Not if it means anything. Well, what did you expect—a nice happy ending? Grow up! Get out of here and into the real world. Go and write your own story because this one . . . this one's history.

[He picks up the CHICKEN.*]*

LUDICRUS: *[To* CHICKEN*]* Here's looking at you, kid.

[Exit LUDICRUS *and the* CHICKEN.*]*

LESSON SIX
EXCUSES

There comes a time in one's career, when the performance is a little below par, or, as we say in theatrical circles—a complete dog's breakfast. The important point here is to remember that it is *never* your fault. When you completely forget your lines, or fall over, or knock the scenery down, you can always blame someone else. The audience, the director, the staging, the acoustics, the government, the price of fish, almost anything can be used.

In the light of this the following excuses might come in useful:

The audience weren't really ready for it.

Actually I meant to fall off the stage. I thought the

piece was too static.
The lights never set the right atmosphere.
I'm more used to the classics.
It was actually a dramatic pause.

And of course, the classic:

The audience didn't notice. They thought it was part of the play.

BIBLIOGRAPHY

Oscar Broompisk:
The Actor and His Body
The Actor and Someone Else's Body
The Actor and Anybody
Using Carrots in the Theatre
Dame Cecily Spume:
Lights, Tights and Lovies—My Life in the Theatre
Great Cravats of the Stage
The Dame Cecily Spume Drama Method Cookbook
Rat Stuffing for Pleasure and Profit
Prof. Hans Liebling:
Shakespeare Revealed—or was the Bard of Avon actually Brian Fothergill of Milton Keynes?
Samuel Tharg:
Using Your Voice as Something to Speak With
Brian Vomit (ed):
Absolutely Everything You Need to Know About Theatre.
Absolutely Everything You Need to Know About Theatre Vol. 2
Cynthia de Larksbottom:
Improvisation and Other Things to do When You Forget the Words
Anton Artaud:
The Theatre of Cruelty
Sergei Meyerstein:
The Theatre of Hatred

Mrs Millicent Fluffybunny:
The Theatre of Being Quite Nice to Each Other and Having Tea Together
Louis Gnomekicker:
Martin Luther—the Man, the Monk, the Stand-Up Comic
Nick Page:
1001 Things to do With Putty

The Greatest Burger Ever Sold

by Nick McIvor

'Jesus, son of Joseph, was born into a working-class family in the provincial town of Nazareth.' So begins the story of the best-known character in history, and yet there are still a host of unanswered questions about his life and work. How was he treated by the press? Where did the disciples go to school? Did his miracles affect health-insurance premiums? *The Greatest Burger Ever Sold* confronts these issues.

The sketches here have appeared at universities and festivals around the country including Mayfest (Glasgow), Greenbelt (Northampton) and York. Described by *The Scotsman* at the 1983 Edinburgh Fringe as 'imaginative', 'brutal', and 'acutely observed', they relate the life of Christ through a series of eye-witnesses who were clearly implied, if not explicitly mentioned in the biblical accounts.

Would Jesus have attracted commercial sponsorship? What did Joseph's mother think? Find out in: *The Greatest Burger Ever Sold.*

NICK McIVOR is an actor, comedian and scriptwriter for stage and television. He lives in London.

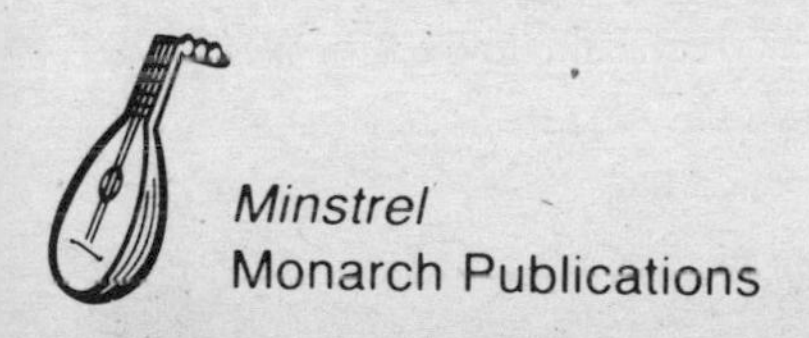
Minstrel
Monarch Publications

The Drama Recipe Book

by Alan MacDonald & Steve Stickley

The Drama Recipe Book offers a mouth-watering array of dramatic dishes. Here are delicious examples of drama as story-telling, role-play, Bible study, street theatre, sermon illustration, worship, workshops and meditation: a succulent variety of sixteen sketches for performance in different contexts.

There is also a thick dollop of cream: games to play, workshop exercises, hints on writing and directing lots of culinary skills to help you prepare memorable dramatic meals. Whether you need to satisfy hungry children, entertain teenagers, prepare a Sunday service or whip up a five-minute assembly single-handed, the recipe is here.

Bon appetit!

ALAN MACDONALD was writer and director for Footprints Theatre Company until 1987. He now lives in Nottingham as a freelance writer.

STEVE STICKLEY is a founder and director of Footprints Theatre Company and has been involved in professional theatre since 1976.

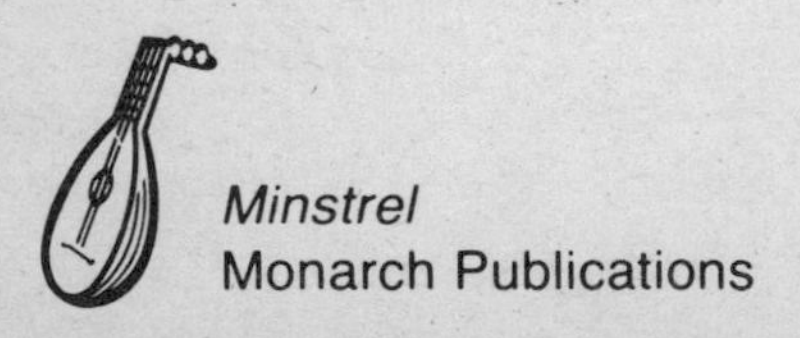
Minstrel
Monarch Publications